THE
SECRET
OF THE
TALPIOT TOMB

UNRAVELLING THE MYSTERY OF
THE JESUS FAMILY TOMB

GARY R. HABERMAS

HOLMAN
REFERENCE

NASHVILLE, TENNESSEE

Holman Reference
B&H Publishing Group
127 Ninth Avenue, North
Nashville, Tennessee 37234
http://www.broadmanholman.com

ISBN: 978-0-8054-9506-5

Designed by Doug Powell

Covers printed in U.S.A. and
text printed and bound in Mexico

DEWEY: 232.97
SUBHD: JESUS CHRIST--RESURRECTION \
APOLOGETICS

1 2 3 4 5 6 7 12 11 10 09 08 07
D

THE SECRET OF
THE TALPIOT TOMB:

UNRAVELLING THE MYSTERY
OF THE JESUS FAMILY TOMB

PREFACE

The bodily resurrection of Jesus from death is and has been a core belief of Christians. This claim on the part of Jesus' followers was challenged immediately and has continued to be challenged. One of the boldest approaches to showing that Jesus' bodily resurrection is myth or a theological embellishment and not fact is the claim that came in early 2007: Odds are 600 to 1 that Jesus' bones have been found in a tomb in a southeast suburb of Jerusalem.

Many have criticized the sensationalism of the documentary and book that make this claim. One of the values of the so-called Talpiot Hypothesis is its clarity and boldness. It's a faith shaker. One believer wrote to Christian philosopher William Lane Craig,

> "My faith has really been shaken by the supposed discovery of Jesus' family tomb. I tell myself this isn't really it, but the nagging doubts remain. Please help me!"

Much help of the kind this believer was seeking has been and is available on the Internet. The number of hits on my own website increased sharply in the days following this announcement. The press soon moved on to other stories as Easter came and went. But for many like the one whose faith was shaken by the discovery of the Jesus' family tomb, they may not have come to a resolution concerning the claim that there's a high probability that Jesus' bones have been found.

In this short volume, I have sought to lay bare the claims of the high probability that Jesus' bones have been found and to assess those claims and the evidence offered for them. Understanding how well these claims stand up to scrutiny can be important not just for evaluating this claim but for knowing the solid evidential ground on which Jesus' bodily resurrection rests. Every believer owes it to himself to understand the case for the resurrection.

THE TALPIOT TOMB AND JEWISH BURIAL PRACTICES

At first almost no one noticed. Israeli archaeologist Amos Kloner reported that on March 28, 1980, the entrance to a Jewish burial tomb was discovered in the East Talpiot region of Jerusalem.[1] At that time, there was no hint of the controversy that would follow later. Actually, little happened or was published on the subject over the next fifteen years. Then during the Easter season of 1996, the BBC broadcast a documentary entitled, "The Body in Question."[2] Still there was not much of a splash.

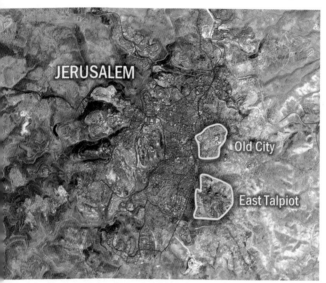

Photo: NASA/GSFC/METI/ERSDAC/JAROS, and U.S./Japan ASTER Science Team

The undisputed facts of the case were quite simple. In the Talpiot Tomb, ten ossuaries, or stone bone boxes, were found, six of which had names inscribed on them. The controversy arose as certain individuals tried to match those names to particular historical figures, including Jesus of Nazareth.

Professional archaeologist Eliot Braun was the first to be dispatched to the site, according to Simcha Jacobovici and Charles Pellegrino. Yosef Gat, an antiquities inspector, went as well. Kloner, another Israeli archaeologist and Ph.D. student, also joined this team of investigators.[3]

Jewish Burial Practices and Jesus' Burial

The Jews required that dead bodies be buried within 24 hours after death. Typically, two sorts of Jewish burial practices were used in the first century A.D. The less common, but better known, involved a burial cave or tomb cut out of the rock that surrounded the city of Jerusalem. Each such tomb included one or more chambers surrounded by rows of loculi, which were burial compartments about the length of a body, also cut into the rock.

First century loculi at Midras. Photo:HolyLandPhotos.org

Each tomb belonged to an extended family and the dead were buried there over several generations. Upon the death of a family member, the dead body was washed, annointed with oil, and then wrapped in a burial shroud. It was then

First century example of a rolling tombstone from Midras, southwest of Jerusalem. Photo:HolyLandPhotos.org

placed in a loculus, with the opening being sealed with a stone slab. Another stone was placed over the outside entrance to the tomb.[4]

The body would lie in the tomb for a year or so, during which time the flesh decayed. When only the person's bones remained in the tomb, they were gathered and placed in a stone ossuary (or bone box) and reburied. In a minority of circumstances—about one quarter of the time—names were then carved on the side of the box. Often more than one person was buried in these bone boxes, seriously complicating the matter of later identifying the remains. These ossuaries were only used for 100 years or so.[5]

BURIAL PROCESS

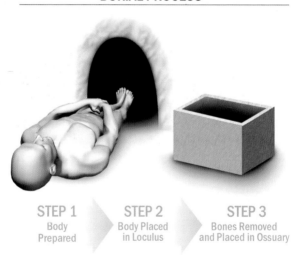

STEP 1	STEP 2	STEP 3
Body Prepared	Body Placed in Loculus	Bones Removed and Placed in Ossuary

Cut stone tombs were very expensive, so the more common way to bury the dead was used chiefly by poorer members of Jewish society. In this case, the majority of the population buried their loved ones in "simple, individual trench graves dug into the ground, similar to the way we bury our dead today." The dirt was then moved back into the trench and a "crude headstone" was usually placed at one end of the burial site to mark the spot. This was not at all dishonorable, but was the most common means of burial. In these cases, nothing would remain to rebury after a year.[6]

Of the two sorts of Jewish burial, the use of the rock tomb is better known today, probably due to the case of Jesus' death and burial. Magness notes that the Gospels are not only our earliest sources, but that they accurately describe the burial by Joseph of Arimathea in a loculus of his family's own tomb. The body had to be buried before the Sabbath began that same day at sundown. Otherwise they would have to wait until Saturday night, after the Sabbath ended. However, that would have exceeded the requirement for burying a dead body within 24 hours. Joseph had to act very quickly.

First century loculi at the Church of the Holy Sepulcher, Jerusalem. Photo:HolyLandPhotos.org

So Joseph procured Jesus' dead body, wrapped it in linen, included spices, and made sure that it was buried hastily late Friday afternoon in his own family tomb. In this, the Gospels show familiarity with Jewish Law.[7]

The Gospels explain that the women returned to see the tomb on Sunday morning. Mark (16:1) and Luke (24:1) specify that they brought spices that they had prepared, apparently to finish Friday afternoon's hasty burial. But all four Gospels teach that when the women arrived, they found the tomb empty. Afterward, the women and others saw the risen Jesus.

The traditional understanding of these events has been challenged by the ossuaries from the Talpiot Tomb. The news dominated the religious world for weeks, beginning days prior to the extended New York press conference on February 27, 2007, followed by the airing of the Discovery Channel documentary on March 4. The latter was followed by a scholarly discussion. In this book we will investigate many challenges, both pro and con, as to whether the claims of the Talpiot Hypothesis can be upheld, over against the New Testament view.

The 2007 press conference promoting the documentary. The Jesus ossuary is on the left, the "Mary Magdalene" ossuary is on the right. Photo: Stan Honda/AFP/Getty Images.

A Word about Sources

To the chagrin of scholars, the Talpiot story has largely been aired in the popular press, from television and radio discussions, to news items, to perhaps hundreds of written publications, often found on the Internet. To be sure, many of these stories and news articles involved scholarly input, sometimes even doing an excellent job of finding the right specialists. Still, many other sources appeared from popular news outlets, as well as on personal and group Web sites. It is not surprising, therefore, that from the beginning this has been a popular story, especially since the original television and book versions were largely associated with the claims of two movie and film producers.

As a mainstream story, much of the information as well as many of the best quotations and critiques have appeared in popular venues. Accordingly, the sources that are employed in this book will be derived from both popular and scholarly areas. We will strive to cite recognized scholars whenever we can, even if the citations are found in popular sources.

Notes

1. Amos Kloner, "A Tomb with Inscribed Ossuaries in East Talpiyot, Jerusalem," 'Atiquot, Vol 29 (1996), 15.
2. James Tabor, *The Jesus Dynasty: The Hidden History of Jesus, His Royal Family, and the Birth of Christianity* (New York: Simon and Schuster, 2006), 23.
3. Simcha Jacobovici and Charles Pellegrino, *The Jesus Family Tomb* (N.Y.: Harper Collins, 2007), 3-8.
4. Jodi Magness, "Has the Tomb of Jesus Been Discovered?" in Society of Biblical Literature Forum, 2007,<http://www.sbl-site.org/Article.aspx?ArticleId=640>(22 March 2007), 2.
5. For details, see Tabor, p. 8. Compare also Joe Zias, "Deconstructing the Second and Hopefully Last Coming of Simcha and the BAR Crowd," March 7, 2007, 2 (joezias.com/tomb.html); Christopher A. Rollston, "Prosopography and the Talpiyot [sic] Yeshua Family Tomb: Pensees of a Paleographer," SBL Forum, March 13, 2007, 3 <http://www.sbl-site.org/Article.aspx?ArticleId=649> (26 March 2007).
6. Magness, 2.
7. Magness, 2-4.

SETTING UP THE DEBATE

The New York news conference, the Discovery Channel documentary, and the publication of the book *The Jesus Family Tomb*[1] made it very plain that James Cameron, Simcha Jacobovici, and Charles Pellegrino thought it very likely that the Talpiot Tomb was indeed the final burial place for the family of Jesus of Nazareth. In this chapter, we will outline the grounds for their argument.

Simcha Jacobovici, James Cameron, and Charles Pellegrino at the 2007 press conference promoting the documentary. The "Mary Magdalene" ossuary is in the foreground. Photo: Stan Honda/AFP/Getty Images.

Incidence of Ossuary Names and DNA Testing

From the very beginning, one of the most confusing aspects of the Talpiot Tomb story was that the names on the six ossuaries looked different from each other. The chief reason is that the names appeared in three different languages: Aramaic, Hebrew, and Greek.

As listed by Kloner, the names are as follows:

A rare variation of Miriam, Maryam or Marya (written in Greek)

Judah son of Jesus (written in Hebrew)

Matthew (written in Hebrew)

Yeshua son of Yehosef ("Jesus, son of Joseph" written in Aramaic)

 A contraction of Yehosef (Joseph) (written in Aramaic)

Mary (written in Hebrew)[2]

Since the Talpiot Tomb, like other rock tombs in Jerusalem, is that of an extended family, DNA analysis would seem to be a natural test. But ossuaries are usually cleaned after discovery, with the contents being reburied. So most of the stone boxes did not have enough material in them to do any DNA testing. As Tabor reported, "the other four inscribed ossuaries had been cleaned/vacuumed and presently have no visible or significant materials that can be tested."[3] This finding was repeated during the Discovery Channel scholarly discussion, hosted by Ted Koppel, with Jacobovici and Tabor both reiterating that only two ossuaries contained enough material to test.[4]

The two ossuaries that still contained material were those of Jesus son of Joseph and Mariamene. These contents were tested in a laboratory at Lakehead University in Ontario, Canada, where researchers were looking for a mitochondrial DNA match-up that would potentially have linked these individuals through a common mother. However, the DNA test came back with negative results.

Arguing that the absence of a DNA match was significant, Jacobovici and Pellegrino concluded that,

11

"Jesus and Mary Magdalene, if their DNA could be read, would be two individuals who had no family ties. But what are the alternatives? People buried in the same tomb were related by either blood or marriage." Thus, since they were not related by blood, they concluded that, most likely, they would have been married.[5]

PREMISE 1: People buried in the same tomb were related by blood or marriage.

PREMISE 2: The contents of the ossuaries labeled Jesus and Mariamene were not related by blood.

CONCLUSION: Therefore, they were related by marriage.

Mary Magdalene and Other Family Connections?

But Jacobovici and Pellegrino go much further than this. Postulating that Jesus and Mariamene were married, they also argue that the latter was really Mary Magdalene, reminiscent of Dan Brown's hypothesis in *The Da Vinci Code*.[6]

Here's how the argument progresses:

※ "Mary" was known in Greek as "Mariamene."

※ Her name was actually written as "Mariamn-u," that is "…of Mariamene."

※ The second portion of the inscription "Mara" is a Greek rendering of an Aramaic word meaning "Lord" or "Master."

※ So the full inscription "of Mariamne" means "also called Lord/Master."

✠ The title on the ossuary is "perfectly consistent with the Mariamne described in the Acts of Philip as the sister of Philip. There she is also explicitly equated with the woman the Gospels called Mary Magdalene."

✠ "The Acts of Philip was widely quoted by early Christian writers but was eventually lost save for a few fragments."

✠ In June 2000, Bovon and Bouvier published the complete translation-into-French of the Mount Athos version of the Acts of Philip, with its identification of Mary Magdalene as "Mariamene," the sister of the apostle Philip.[7]

NO DNA MATCH THEREFORE PROBABLY MARRIED SINCE THEY WERE IN FAMILY TOMB TOGETHER

YESHUA SON OF YEHOSEF

MARIAMENE

THUS JUDE MUST BE THEIR SON

YEHUDA SON OF YESHUA

Therefore, since "Jesus the son of Joseph" was not related by blood to "Mariamene," then they must have been married. And since Mariamene is probably Mary Magdalene, as just indicated by the argument above, then the "Judah son of Jesus" who is also buried in another ossuary in the same tomb must be their son.[8] Other probable connections to the Holy Family can also be made. The other Mary was probably Jesus' mother and the Joseph in Jesus' tomb was his father. "Yose" (Jose) was probably Jesus' brother (which is spelled similarly in Mark 6:3), rather than a nickname for Joseph.

The name "Matthew" is similar to some of the names of Jesus' ancestors (Luke 3:23-25).

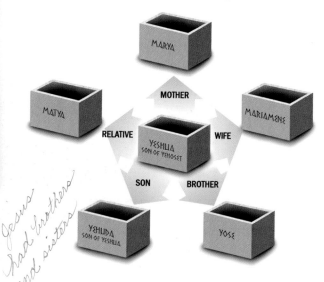

A last probability, according to the Talpiot Hypothesis researchers, pertains to the "missing ossuary" that came out of the tomb. Although there were originally ten ossuaries in the tomb, later inventories showed that one of them was missing; it was not with the others. So it has been asserted that this missing box might actually be the famous "James son of Joseph brother of Jesus" ossuary. This, of course, would argue for even tighter family connections.

As Tabor remarked even a year ago, "I noticed that the dimensions of the missing tenth ossuary are precisely the same, to the centimeter, to those of the James Ossuary." Perhaps Oded Golan, the owner of the James ossuary who went to trial on the supposition that he received the James ossuary illegally, actually found the James ossuary not in the 1970s, as he claims, but about 1980, "when the Talpiot tomb was discovered?"[9]

The James Ossuary. Photo: Biblical Archaeology Society of Washington, D.C./Getty Images.

Perhaps a little less sure, Jacobovici and Pellegrino argue that, while not precisely the same, the James ossuary is of similar size to the measurements that were taken of the missing tenth ossuary. "So, the missing ossuary and the James ossuary may be one and the same after all."[10]

In order to test further this possibility that the two ossuaries are the same, last July 31, 2006, a series of tests were conducted on random ossuary samples that had been collected in Israel.

A farmer in the Hill Country of Judea working terra rossa. Photo: HolyLandPhotos.org

Patina is a substance that forms on metal as a result of exposure to nature. The green tint on the Statue of Liberty is a result of patination.

A reddish soil type—terra rossa—is found in the hills around Jerusalem. It is rarer and more red than some other soils, and contains a high iron content. According to the tests, "This was all consistent with the patinas on the James and Talpiot tomb ossuaries." While most of the ossuaries tested differently, "compared to other patina samples from ossuaries found in the Jerusalem environment, the Talpiot tomb ossuaries exhibited a patina fingerprint or profile that matched the James ossuary and no other."[11]

Another possibility exists, too. Tabor credits Shimon Gibson as first suggesting that the James ossuary might not have been the tenth ossuary at all, but merely another one that may have been stolen from the Talpiot Tomb the first weekend when the tomb was left open.[12]

So the Talpiot Hypothesis holds that the Talpiot Tomb is the burial site of Jesus of Nazareth's family. Marya is Jesus' mother and Joseph is his father. Mariamene is Mary Magdalene, Jesus' wife, and Judah is their son. Jose is Jesus' brother, not his father. And his brother James was probably also buried in this same tomb.

Statisical Analysis: Jesus' Tomb?

On the surface at least, and with a couple of potential exceptions, the family names in the Talpiot Tomb seem to fit nicely with the known family members in Jesus of Nazareth's household. Is there any way to be more specific about whether or not we could have a potential match here?

To check out their hunch, Jacobovici and

Pellegrino sought the services of Andre Feuerverger, a statistician from the University of Toronto. While most of the Talpiot names are very common, what is the likelihood that just this particular cluster of names would all be together?

Tabor explains that the initial statistics for the Talpiot grouping have nothing to do with whether or not they fit the family of Jesus of Nazareth. Rather, they were arrived at in a two-part process. First, what is the likelihood that such a cluster of names would be found in one place or in a single family? Second, these findings then were compared to Jesus' family according to the names presented in the Gospels.[13]

Based on the available information and the family connections mentioned above, Feuerverger arrived at the following figures for this cluster of names alone: there is a 1 in 190 chance of having a Jesus son of Joseph, a 1 in 160 chance for Mariamne, a 1 in 40 chance for Matia, a 1 in 20 chance for Yose, and a 1 in 4 chance for Maria. Multiplying these odds yields a likelihood of 1 chance in 97,280,000 of getting this specific list of persons together.

What about his brother's? HA!

$$\frac{1}{190} \times \frac{1}{160} \times \frac{1}{40} \times \frac{1}{20} \times \frac{1}{4} = \frac{1}{97,280,000}$$

Then the second set of computations was done, comparing the family buried in the Talpiot Tomb to the Gospel listings of Jesus of Nazareth's family members. The name "Matthew" was eliminated during this step, because he is not explicatively mentioned in the Gospels as a direct member of Jesus' family. Then other adjustments were made for unintentional biases in the historical sources, as well as to allow for all possible first-century Jerusalem tombs, arriving at a final probability factor of a 1 in 600 chance that the Talpiot Tomb was not the family tomb of Jesus of Nazareth. So the conclusion was that the two families were probably the same, to a very high degree of likelihood, and thus Jesus is probably buried in this tomb.[14]

Tabor's Summary of the Argument

James Tabor recently provided a very helpful summary of the arguments in favor of what we have called the Talpiot Hypothesis. I have attempted to categorize the arguments under his twofold division as stated above, looking first at the Talpiot data, and then comparing it to the family of Jesus of Nazareth.

First are the findings from the Talpiot Tomb:

- "Nothing like this [statistical grouping of names] occurs anywhere else." This is especially so when we consider that the names were discovered as belonging "in one family."

- To illustrate the statistical likelihood of these names being together in a single family, Tabor uses a range of population figures for Second Temple Jerusalem, estimating that between 25,000 and 75,000 people lived in the city. Consulting with several statisticians, he then compares Jerusalem to a football stadium filled

  with 50,000 persons, including men, women, and children. In that group, an estimated 2,796 men, would be named Jesus. Of these, 351 would have a Joseph for a father and 173 of them would also have a mother named Mary. Only 23 of these men named Jesus would also have a brother named Joseph. If we also added having a brother named James, we would be left with only one person named Jesus. This presumes a "modest pre-70 CE family burial cave" with a "tighter time span" than three generations.

Then we compare these figures to the family of Jesus of Nazareth:

✠ Jesus' father Joseph probably died earlier and so he would have been buried in Galilee.

✠ Jesus' four brothers also seem to fit the Talpiot Tomb scenario, too. Simon and Jude probably lived past A.D. 70, but Jesus and James died before then. The simple interpretation is that "Jose" is Jesus' brother, rather than his father, and is also the one buried in the Talpiot ossuary. *Simon + Jude may have been older in age.*

✠ Of the two "Marys" buried in the tomb, we have "the likelihood that Maria could well be the mother" of Jesus.

✠ There is also the "logical possibility" that "Mariamene" is Mary Magdalene, as indicated by "several early Christian texts" like the Gospel of Mary, Hippolytus, and the Acts of Philip, and based on research regarding Mary Magdalene's "place in earliest history of the Jesus movement."

✠ If Judah is Jesus' son, then "Mariamene" is "a likely candidate" for being Judah's mother, although we really "have no way of knowing" for sure.

✠ Matthew could be a family member.

✠ Tabor's conclusion regarding the evidence is that it is "possible-to-likely" that the Talpiot Tomb is that of the Jesus of Nazareth family. But if the supposition is correct that the James ossuary was also in the Talpiot Tomb, then Tabor thinks that this would make the identification "close to certain."[15]

Conclusion: Jesus' Spiritual Resurrection and Ascension?

Those who hold the Talpiot Hypothesis seem to favor the conclusion that it is highly likely that this tomb contains the bones of Jesus of Nazareth and his family. Of the group, Tabor is the most cautious, claiming that this scenario is "possible-to-likely." But since Tabor also thinks that it is likely that the James ossuary did come from the Talpiot Tomb, it would seem that he, too, believes that the entire hypothesis is "close to certain."[16]

An intriguing issue is that Jacobovici has been reported many times as stating that these conclusions should not bother or offend Christians! He maintains this stance because he does not deny Jesus' resurrection or ascension to heaven, for these events could have happened spiritually. However, he does note that Christians who believe that Jesus rose bodily from the dead, or later ascended bodily to heaven would have issues with his conclusions.[17]

For example, the report on the Discovery Channel, in bold print, said:

I am offended.

Even if Jesus' body was moved from one tomb to another, however, that does not mean that he could not have been resurrected from the second tomb. Belief in the resurrection is based not on which tomb he was buried in, but on alleged sightings of Jesus that occurred after his burial and documented in the Gospels.[18]

He was placed in a borrowed tomb.

The report continues with regard to Jesus' ascension:

Some Christians believe that this was a *spiritual* ascension, i.e., his mortal remains were left behind. Other Christians believe that he ascended *with* his body to heaven. **If Jesus' mortal remains have been found, this would contradict the idea of a physical ascension but not the idea of a spiritual** ascension. **The latter is consistent with Christian theology.**[19] *yes,*

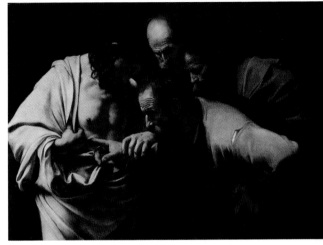

The Incredulity of Saint Thomas by Caravaggio

Tabor also stated his belief that the resurrection was not a material, bodily event, but a "spiritual resurrection."[20] Tabor develops this thesis, arguing chiefly that Paul held to less than bodily resurrection appearances, like the one he experienced. "God then raised Christ from the dead and transformed him back into his glorious heavenly body." Further, Christians will also experience such a resurrection, with their bodies being "instantaneously changed from flesh to spirit." It is only later that the Gospels portrayed Jesus' appearances as bodily in nature.[21]

Many scholars have reacted strongly against these ideas. The arguments on behalf of the Talpiot Hypothesis will be addressed in much detail in the next two chapters.

Notes:

1. Simcha Jacobovici and Charles Pellegrino, *The Jesus Family Tomb* (San Francisco: Harper Collins, 2007).

2. Amos Kloner, "A Tomb with Inscribed Ossuaries in East Talpiyot, Jerusalem," 'Atiqout, Vol. 29 (1996), pp. 17-19. Cf. also Christopher A. Rollston, "Prosopography and the Talpiyot Yeshua Family Tomb: Pensees of a Palaeographer," SBL Forum, 2007, <http://www.sbl-site.org/Article.aspx?ArticleId=649> (26 March 2007); James Tabor, *The Jesus Dynasty: The Hidden History of Jesus, His Royal Family, and the Birth of Christianity* (N.Y.: Simon and Schuster, 2006), p. 23.

3. James Tabor, "DNA and the Talpiot Ossuaries," Jesus Dynasty Blog, 2007, http://jesusdynasty.com/blog/2007/03/13/dna-and-thetalpiot-ossuaries/

4. Discovery Channel Interview, "The Lost Tomb of Jesus: A Critical Look," March 4, 2007, chaired by Ted Koppel.

5. Jacobovici and Pellegrino, 168. Cf. also Stuart Laidlaw, "Christ's Tomb Found? Canadian Filmmaker Claims Burial Boxes Belonged to Christ's Family," Toronto Star, February 25, 2007, 2.

6. Dan Brown, *The Da Vinci Code: A Novel* (N.Y.: Doubleday, 2003), Chapters 56, 58.

7. Jacobovici and Pellegrino, see especially 76, 95.

8. For another similarity here, see Brown, 249.

9. Tabor, *The Jesus Dynasty*, 33.

10. Jacobovici and Pellegrino, 210.

11. Jacobovici and Pellegrino, 182, 188.

12. Tabor's email to colleagues, February 28, 2007, 1-2.

13. Tabor's email to colleagues, February 28, 2007, 2-3.

14. "Statistics Overview" from Andrey Feuerverger's analysis, Discovery Channel Website.

15. Tabor,"The Jesus Dynasty Blog," March 24, 2007, 1-4.

16. Ibid., 3-4.

17. Laidlaw, "Christ's Tomb Found?," 1-2.

18. "Theological Considerations," Discovery Channel.

19. Ibid., The italics are original, and the last two sentences were written in bold type.

20. Discovery Channel Interview, "The Lost Tomb of Jesus: A Critical Look," March 4, 2007, chaired by Ted Koppel.

21. Tabor, *The Jesus Dynasty*, 230-233, 262-266; both quotations are from page 264.

FAMILY NAMES,
MARY MAGDALENE,
THE JAMES OSSUARY,
AND DNA

The Talpiot Hypothesis began to circulate and gain attention, popularized by the initial news conference, the Discovery Channel documentary, the book by Jacobovici and Pellegrino, and the seemingly countless interviews, articles, and news items. Most of the major news television networks and news periodicals reported the arguments, pro and con. Biblical scholars entered the discussion at a torrid pace. Interestingly, much of the response came from non-evangelical scholars who plainly set themselves against the Talpiot claims.[1]

Entrance to the Talpiot Tomb. Photo: Professor Amos Kloner, Courtesy of Israel Antiquities Authority via Getty Images.

In this chapter we will address several of the major portions of the Talpiot Hypothesis. Here we will concentrate on the issues regarding the family names, the possibility of a Mariamene/Mary Magdalene identification, the "other" ossuary, and the DNA testing. Our format will be to isolate the key questions, as set out in chapter 2, and then provide lists of the scholarly counter-arguments. Endnotes provide a wide variety of sources for these responses. Hopefully, the reader will then be in a position to judge the strength of each claim and response.

How common are the names found in the Talpiot Tomb?
Virtually all commentators, including those who agree with the Talpiot thesis, agree that most of the names in the tomb were very commonly found in first-century Jerusalem.

Tal Ilan, compiler of the *Lexicon of Jewish Names* "disagreed vehemently" with the view that the Talpiot Tomb was Jesus' burial place, and said that these names "are in every tomb in Jerusalem . . . you could expect to find them everywhere."[2]

Ossuaries found on the grounds of Dominus Flevit on the Mount of Olives. Photo: HolyLandPhotos.org.

Stephen Pfann argues from L.Y. Rahmani's *A Catalog of Jewish Ossuaries*, that every one of the names for Jesus' family members is found in the list of the most popular 16 male and female names.

Four of those names (Simon, Mary, Joseph, and Judas) are among the top five male and female names in frequency and comprise 38 percent of the entire list! Jesus is the seventh most common male name.[3]

- Richard Bauckham notes that the name Joseph is found on 45 ossuaries, while the name Jesus is found on 22 ossuaries. "Mary" is found on 42 ossuaries.[4]

- Even the particular congruence of names in the Talpiot Tomb is not absolutely unique. Near the Mount of Olives, another burial tomb reportedly lists a number of ossuaries also inscribed in Hebrew, Aramaic, and Greek. The names include Jesus, Joseph, Mary, Martha, and Matthew.[5]

Can we even be sure of the name "Jesus" on the Talpiot ossuary? In the first place, it's not even clear that the name on the ossuary is "Jesus." Here is a facsimile of the inscription:

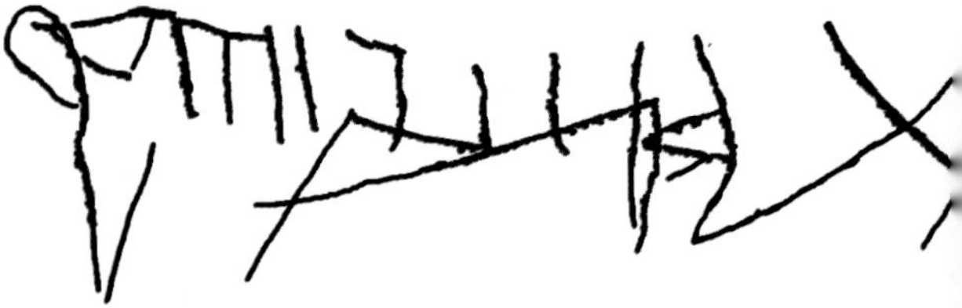

One can make out the words "son of Joseph" but the initial name on the right is like a child's scrawl with a crayon on the wall. It may not be "Jesus" at all.

- James Charlesworth, cited in the Talpiot presentation, states that the name "Jesus" before that of "Joseph" on that particular ossuary "is the most difficult name to read among all the names in the tomb." He adds, "The scribbling is not an inscription, it is sloppy graffiti."[6]

✠ Pfann is not sure that the name is Jesus. He thinks that "it's more likely the name `Hanun.'"[7]

✠ Steve Caruso argues that "I cannot be even 10 percent conclusive about anything else in this inscription other than the name `Joseph.'"[8]

✠ Tabor even acknowledges that the name "Jesus" is "nearly illegible."[9]

Mariamene and Mary Magdalene

Was Mariamene another name for Mary Magdalene?

✠ There are no good historical reasons to trace the name "Mariamene" to Mary Magdalene.

✼ Sources dating from the middle to late third to fifth centuries like Hippolytus, the Gospel of Mary, and the Acts of Phillip are far too late to be helpful with historical questions pertaining to the life, death, and resurrection of Jesus.[10] It is amazing that Tabor refers to these sources as "several early Christian texts" and the "earliest history of the Jesus movement" while holding that the Gospels are often too late to be helpful![11]

✼ Further, even in Hippolytus (in "Refutation of All Heresies") and the Acts of Phillip (dated by Bauckham to the late fourth to the early fifth century), the person "Mariamene" is never specifically identified as Mary Magdalene. Although Mariamene is mentioned several times in the Acts of Phillip, Joseph Fitzmeyer states that "there is not one instance that suggests she is Mary of Magdala."[12] Witherington adds that in Hippolytus, the name is not even the same as on the Talpiot ossuary.[13]

- Fitzmyer thinks that this lack of identification is the "biggest problem" for the claims by Jacobovici and Pellegrino. For example, the "ou" ending of the name "Mariamenou" is actually masculine/neuter, so how could it even be a woman's name? For these and other reasons, "the whole account about 'the Jesus family tomb' loses its most crucial piece of 'evidence.'"[14]

- Further, "Mara" does not mean Master or Teacher, but is short for Martha. Joseph Fitzmyer calls the Talpiot thesis translation a gratuitous assumption.[15]

- Witherington says that Mary was known as being from Magdal or Magdala. Without that geographical designation, the name is far too common to tie to Mary Magdalene.[16]

"THERE IS NOT ONE INSTANCE THAT SUGGESTS SHE IS MARY OF MAGDALA."

JOSEPH FITZMYER

What could the ossuary name "Mariamene" indicate?

- Bauckham thinks that the woman buried in the ossuary probably had two names: "Mariamenon" (Greek) and "Mara" (Semitic). Since the former is "a term of endearment" it probably indicates a bilingual family that spoke Greek at home, another problem for identifying this as Jesus' family.[17]

✠ Witherington also concludes that the ossuary probably contained the remains of two women, or a woman and child, or one woman with two names. Perhaps favoring the two persons view is that there appears to be a "slash line" between the names. Still, none of these names is that of Mary Magdalene.[18]

> "I MUST SAY THAT THE RECONSTRUCTIONS OF JESUS' MARRIAGE WITH MARY MAGDALENE AND THE BIRTH OF A CHILD BELONG FOR ME TO SCIENCE FICTION."[22]
>
> FRANÇOIS BOVON

> "THERE IS NO REASON AT ALL TO CONNECT THE WOMAN IN THIS OSSUARY WITH MARY MAGDALENE, AND IN FACT THE NAME USAGE IS DECISIVELY AGAINST SUCH A CONNEXION (SIC)."[21]
>
> RICHARD BAUCKHAM

> "NO REPUTABLE HISTORIAN OF CHRISTIAN ORIGINS SERIOUSLY THINKS THAT JESUS WAS MARRIED TO MARY MAGDALENE (OR ANYONE ELSE, AS FAR AS WE KNOW)."[23]
>
> MARK GOODACRE

✠ Pfann concludes that the "Mariamene" ossuary is really that of two persons: "Mariame" and ("kai") "Mara," the latter being added to the ossuary later.[19] Tabor responded to Pfann that a specialist, Di Segni, thinks Pfann is mistaken and still holds to the view that Mariamene is a double name for a single woman buried in the ossuary.[20]

- Baukham concludes: "There is no reason at all to connect the womain in the ossuary with Mary Magdalene, and in fact the name usage is decisively against such a connexion (sic)."[21]

The bottom line is that scholars have uniformly rejected the suggestion that Mariamene is Mary Magdalene.

Was Jesus married? Did he have children?

- Harvard scholar Francois Bovon, whose work on Mary Magdalene is cited by Tabor and the Talpiot Hypothesis thesis, still concludes, "I must say that the reconstructions of Jesus' marriage with Mary Magdalene and the birth of a child belong for me to science fiction."[22]

- Mark Goodacre of Duke University adds that "no reputable historian of Christian origins seriously thinks that Jesus was married to Mary Magdalene (or anyone else, as far as we know)."[23]

- It would seem that in theological terms, nothing negative would follow either from Jesus being married or his fathering children. It could be true even if the New Testament never recorded it. After all, it was normal for first-century Jews to marry and if this were the case, Jesus would be the model for husband-wife relations, as well as fatherhood! So there is no need to disregard these hypotheses for such reasons. However, the chief problem is not the theoretical concept itself, but the revisionist history that is the main ally of these ideas, as it attempts to invent this thesis without any evidence.

- Not one ancient historical source claims that Jesus was married, either to Mary Magdalene or to anyone else. Neither are there any ancient historical sources that teach that Jesus had children.

- There are several considerations in the New Testament that appear to argue against the claim that Jesus was married, although it probably should be acknowledged that none of these proves the case, either. As just indicated, Jesus' wife is never mentioned, even though it would be normal. Arguments from silence are notoriously weak, so we cannot place too much emphasis on this point, but it is worth mentioning. Jesus' teaching about being single for the kingdom of heaven's sake (Matt. 19:12) is also a pointer.

- If Jesus had been married, this would have been a wonderful clincher to Paul's argument that apostles have the right to bring their wives with them in ministry, although the best Paul could do was to refer to Peter and Jesus' brothers (1 Cor. 9:5). That would have clinched Paul's argument by itself![24]

- Acts 8:30-34 implies that Jesus had no descendants. At the cross, Jesus committed his mother to John, not to his son (John 19:26). Jesus' brother James is the leader of early church in Jerusalem (Acts 15). But since there is no evidence at all that Jesus was married, it should not be necessary to mention his lack of offspring!

- Goodacre states that the available evidence argues that Jesus did not have a son. It will not do to postulate otherwise without historical data by saying that "our evidence is incomplete," or that we should be open to it, or simply that we cannot rule out the possibility.[25] Positive evidence is needed.

The James Ossuary. Photo: Biblical Archaeology Society of Washington, D.C./Getty Images.

The Missing Tenth Ossuary

Was the missing ossuary from Talpiot the same as the James ossuary?

✠ This entire discussion assumes and depends on the assertion that the James ossuary is itself authentic, which is highly disputed.[26] If it is a fake, this issue is a moot point. Or even if the ossuary is authentic, but the words "brother of Jesus" have been added, as some have charged, then the Talpiot Hypothesis is weakened considerably.

✠ The James ossuary appears in a 1976 photo produced by Oded Golan (owner of James ossuary) at his trial.[27] Reportedly, former FBI agent Gerald Richard testified in the Israeli court proceedings that the photo came from Golan's home and did indeed date to the 1970s, as indicated by tests performed in the FBI photo lab.[28] Jacobovici has even admitted that if the James ossuary was photographed in the 1970s, it could not be from a tomb that was discovered in 1980, the date of the Talpiot Tomb find.[29]

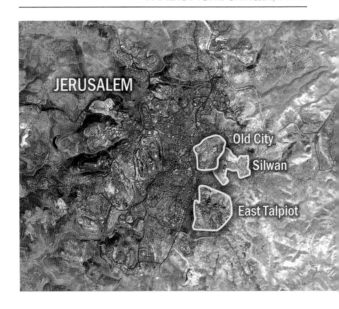

The dealer who supplied Oded Golan with the James ossuary said that it came from Silwan, not Talpiot. The dirt found in the ossuary backs up that claim.[30] Plus, Silwan is within sight of the temple, as required by the Eusebius citation below.[31]

According to ancient historian Eusebius (*Ecclesiastical History* 2:23), James was buried on the same location where he was stoned, near the temple. This is not near the Talpiot location.[32]

The martyrdom of James, illustrated by Jan Luiken in the 1685 edition of the *Martyr's Mirror*. Courtesy of the Mennonite Library at Bethel College.

✠ Amos Kloner and Joe Zias disagree with James Tabor regarding the tenth ossuary: Amos Kloner retrieved the tenth ossuary and Joe Zias catalogued it at the Rockefeller Museum while he was the curator there. As the original scholars who did the work, they clarified the issue as follows:[33]

❀ The measurements of the tenth Talpiot ossuary are significantly different from that of the James ossuary. The James ossuary measures 50.5cm x 25cm x 30.5cm, while the tenth ossuary measured 60cm x 26cm x 30cm, with the latter measurements appearing in Kloner's original article, years ago.[34] So the tenth Talpiot ossuary is 20 percent longer than the James ossuary.

❀ There was no name on the tenth ossuary—it was plain. So it was not even photographed. Plain ossuaries without inscriptions or ornaments were then placed in the inner courtyard of Rockefeller Museum while Zias was the curator there, and that is where the tenth box was taken. So it was not the James ossuary.

❀ Stephen Goranson of Duke University states that Tabor has known of the discrepancy between his view and the Kloner/Zias view, at least since November 23, 2006, after complaining about Goranson's writing in the *Jerusalem Perspective*.[35]

✠ Tabor acknowledges straightforwardly: "I am not sure if the 10th ossuary is or is not the one we now know as the 'James ossuary.'" But he still thinks that when Kloner wrote his original article in 1996, that "he had nothing to go on but the registration number and dimensions, so he writes 'plain.'" If Kloner did see and remember the tenth ossuary, "that is for him to say."[36]

So far, scholarship has sided firmly with the work of Kloner and Zias, and against the hypothesis that the tenth ossuary is that of James the brother of Jesus. Goodacre concludes: "At this point it looks highly unlikely that the James ossuary is the missing tenth box from the Talpiot tomb, unless the data we possess requires correction"[37] Jonathan Reed stated: "I do not think Kloner would have missed that; I refuse to believe it."[38] Witherington concurs with the reports of Kloner and Zias, including some personal e-mails from the latter.[39] The almost uniform view is that the tenth ossuary was never missing or stolen; it has been accounted for since the beginning. But since it had no name on it and the dimensions are significantly different, it is very probably not the James ossuary.

Do the patinas match on the Talpiot ossuaries and the James box?

 Zias charges that the film shows experts "scraping material from the ossuary, under the worst possible conditions." So Zias concludes that the "experts" involved in this testing "have no expertise whatsoever with local materials"—one was reportedly an authority in auto crashes![40]

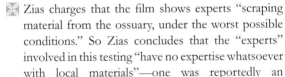

Details showing the patinas of the James ossuary (left) and the Jesus ossuary (right). Photos: Left: Drew Cunningham/Getty Images Right: Mariana Salzberger, Courtesy of Israel Antiquities Authority via Getty Images.

✠ Witherington says about the comparison of patinas: "This is not actually surprising [sic] at all since you can find terra rosa in various locales in and around Jerusalem."[41]

✠ Ted Koppel reported: "We called Robert Genna at the Suffolk County Crime Lab and he said: 'The elemental composition of some of the samples we tested from the ossuaries are consistent with each other. But I would never say they are a match . . . . No scientist would ever say definitively that one ossuary came from the same tomb as another . . .'"[42]

The DNA Testing

✠ A devastating problem for DNA testing is that multiple skeletons were often placed in the same ossuary. For instance, Joe Zias published the results of one tomb he investigated where 15 ossuaries contained the remains of 88 people![43] More crucially for our purposes, in his original article, investigating archaeologist Amos Kloner estimated that there were 35 different people in the Talpiot Tomb--17 in the ossuaries and 18 outside the ossuaries.[44] Tabor disputes the presence of 35 people in the Talpiot Tomb, arguing that in the original report by Joseph Gath, there were two or three people outside the ossuaries and "a dozen or so" inside the bone boxes.[45] But even without arguing the specifics, Tabor's total of 14-18 people still makes the point sufficiently well. Thus, Christopher Rollston rightly

Bones found in a ossuary. Photo: John Phillips//Time Life Pictures/Getty Images

notes that, "because of the numbers of burials in the tombs, the practice of interring the skeletal remains of multiple people in a single ossuary, and the possibility of contamination of laboratory data, the notion that decisive data can be produced seems to me to be most difficult."[46] Indeed, without knowing whose bones we are testing, what good is DNA?

✠ Further, besides the presence of other persons in the same ossuaries, DNA testing could record the presence of anyone who came in contact with the bone boxes, including Joe Zias himself![47]

> "THE ONLY CONCLUSIONS WE MADE WAS THAT [SIC] THESE TWO SETS WERE NOT MATERNALLY RELATED. TO ME IT SOUNDS LIKE ABSOLUTELY NOTHING."
> CARNEY MATHESON

✠ Witherington states that the lack of a DNA control sample is another huge issue—we need a sample from a member of Jesus' family. But without such, DNA may say that certain persons were related (although not this time!), but they could never say that they belonged to Jesus or anyone else in Jesus' family. But we do not have this family DNA evidence and never will.[48] Even Tabor agrees here: "Such tests, no matter what the results, could not 'prove' that this particular Jesus was the one who became known as Christ but can only show relations between the persons buried in the tomb."[49]

✠ Carney Matheson, who performed the DNA test on the "Jesus" and "Mariamene" ossuaries, stated,

"The only conclusions we made was [sic] that these two sets were not maternally related. To me it sounds like absolutely nothing."[50]

Conclusion

In this chapter we have addressed several aspects of the Talpiot Hypothesis. In particular, we have responded to the claims regarding the commonality of the Talpiot Tomb names, the identification of an ossuary believed by a few to be that of Mary Magdalene, the question of the tenth ossuary, and the DNA testing. On each count, we have discovered no basis for the claims that this is the burial tomb of Jesus of Nazareth's family. The remainder of the claims will be addressed in the next chapter.

Notes:
1. For details of this scholarly outcry, see Appendix 1.
2. Christopher Mims, "Special Report: Has James Cameron Found Jesus's Tomb or Is It Just a Statistical Error?" *Scientific American*, March 2, 2007, 3.
3. Stephen Pfann, "The Improper Application of Statistics in 'The Lost Tomb of Jesus,' " (University of the Holy Land, 1-2).
4. Richard Bauckham, "The Alleged 'Jesus Family Tomb,' " March 1, 2007, 2; found at http://www.christilling.de/blog/ctblog.html, downloaded on March 1, 2007); Bauckham's ossuary statistics are also listed in Ben Witherington, "The Jesus Tomb? 'Titanic' Talpiot Tomb Theory Sunk from the Start," February 26, 2007 (http://benwitherington.blogspot.com/, downloaded on February 26, 2007). See also Joe Zias, "Deconstructing the Second and Hopefully Last Coming of Simcha and the BAR Crowd," 2-3; found at http://www.joezias.com/tomb.html, downloaded on March 6, 2007.
5. "Dominus Flevit," 2 (downloaded on March 22, 2007); email from Michael S. Heiser, March 13, 2007.
6. James H. Charlesworth, "Reflections on the So-called 'Lost Tomb of Jesus,' " February 7, 2007, 1.

7. Karen Matthews, "Documentary Shows Possible Jesus Tomb," Associated Press, February 26, 20007, 2.

8. "The Aramaic Blog," February 29, 2007, 3; also listed on "NT Gateway" site of Mark Goodacre of Duke University.

9. Tabor, *The Jesus Dynasty*, 23.

10. Bauckham, "The Alleged 'Jesus Family Tomb,'" 3-4; Pfann, "The Improper Application of Statistics in 'The Lost Tomb of Jesus,'" 3; Ben Witherington, "Problems Multiply for Jesus Tomb Theory," February 28, 2007, 2 (http://benwitherington.blogspot.com/, downloaded on February 28, 2007).

11. James Tabor, "The Talpiot Jesus Tomb: An Overview," The Jesus Dynasty Blog, March 24, 2007, 3.

12. Joseph Fitzmyer, book review of Simcha Jacobovici and Charles Pellegrino, The Jesus Family Tomb in America: *The National Catholic Weekly*, date?, 3 (downloaded on April 2, 2007); Witherington, "Problems Multiply for Jesus Tomb Theory," 2.

13. Ben Witherington, "The Jesus Tomb Show—Biblical Archaeologists Reject Discovery Channel Show's Claims," March 5, 2007, 3.

14. Fitzmyer, book review, 2-3.

15. Fitzmyer, book review, 2; Witherington, "Problems Multiply for Jesus Tomb Theory," 2.

16. Witherington, "The Jesus Tomb? 'Titanic' Talpiot Tomb Theory Sunk from the Start," 4.

17. Bauckham, "The Alleged 'Jesus Family Tomb,'" 5.

18. Witherington, "The Jesus Tomb? 'Titanic' Talpiot Tomb Theory Sunk from the Start," 3; "Problems Multiply for Jesus Tomb Theory," 3-4, 6-7.

19. Stephen Pfann, "Mary Magdalene is Now Missing: A Corrected Reading of Rahmani Ossuary 701," *Society of Biblical Literature Forum*, March, 2007, 7.

20. James Tabor, "Tabor Responds to Phann," *Society of Biblical Literature Forum*, March, 2007, 1.

21. Bauckham, "The Alleged 'Jesus Family Tomb,'" 5.

22. Francois Bovon, "The Tomb of Jesus," *Society of Biblical Literature Forum*, March, 2007, 1.

23. Mark Goodacre, "The Statistical Case for the Identity of the "Jesus Family Tomb," NT Gateway, March 1, 2007, 1.

24. Michael Licona, "First Person: Has the Family Tomb of

Jesus Been Found?" BP News, February 27, 2007, 1-3.

25. Mark Goodacre, "The Statistical Case for the Identity of the "Jesus Family Tomb," March 1, 2007, 2.

26. Zias, "Deconstructing the Second and Hopefully Last Coming of Simcha and the BAR Crowd," 2.

27. For examples of those who mention this, see Zias, "Deconstructing the Second and Hopefully Last Coming of Simcha and the BAR Crowd," 2-3; Chris Rosebrough, "Archaeological Identity Theft: The Lost Tomb of Jesus Fails to Make the Grade," Extreme Theology, 3; http://www.extremetheology.com/, downloaded on February 27, 2007.

28. Stuart Laidlaw, "Christ's Tomb Found? Canadian Filmmaker Claims Burial Boxes Belonged to Christ's Family," Toronto Star, February 25, 2007, 3.

29. Ibid., 3.

30. Witherington, "The Jesus Tomb? 'Titanic' Talpiot Tomb Theory Sunk from the Start," 5.

31. Witherington, "Problems Multiply for Jesus Tomb Theory," 5.

32. Witherington, "The Jesus Tomb? 'Titanic' Talpiot Tomb Theory Sunk from the Start," 5; Licona, "First Person: Has the Family Tomb of Jesus Been Found?" 1).

33. Kloner, "A Tomb with Inscribed Ossuaries in East Talpiot," 15-22; David Horovitz, Question and Answer interview with Amos Kloner, "Kloner: A Great Story, but Nonsense," *Jerusalem Post*, February 27, 2007, 1; Zias, "Deconstructing the Second and Hopefully Last Coming of Simcha and the BAR Crowd," 2-4); personal emails from Joe Zias, March 1, 2007 and from Amos Kloner, March 3, 2007.

34. Kloner, "A Tomb with Inscribed Ossuaries in East Talpiot," 21.

35. Goranson as quoted by Mark Goodacre, NT Gateway Weblog, February 27, 2007, 1-2.

36. Tabor comment from February 27, 2007 as quoted in Christopher Heard, "They're Baaaa-aaaack," February 25, 2007, 2-3. (http://www.heardworld.com/higgaion/?p=539, downloaded on February 28, 2007.

37. Mark Goodacre, NT Gateway Weblog, February 27, 2007, 2.

38. Jonathan Reed, Discovery Channel Interview with Ted Koppel, "The Lost Tomb of Jesus: A Critical Look," March 4, 2007.

39. Ben Witherington, "The Smoking Gun---Tenth Talpiot Ossuary Proved to be Blank," March 1, 2007, 1-2.

40. Zias, "Deconstructing the Second and Hopefully Last Coming of Simcha and the BAR Crowd," 2.

41. Witherington, "Problems Multiply for Jesus Tomb Theory," 4.

42. Ted Koppel, Discovery Channel Interview, "The Lost Tomb of Jesus: A Critical Look."

43. Zias, "Deconstructing the Second and Hopefully Last Coming of Simcha and the BAR Crowd," 2-3.

44. Amos Kloner, "A Tomb with Inscribed Ossuaries in East Talpiyot [sic], Jerusalem," `Antiqot, Vol 29 (1996), especially note 2, 22.

45. Tabor, "The Talpiot Jesus Tomb: An Overview," The Jesus Dynasty Blog, March 24, 2007, 2.

46. Christopher A. Rollston, "Prosopography and the Talpiyot [sic] Yeshua Family Tomb: Pensees of a Paleographer," Society of Biblical Literature Forum, March, 2007, endnote 29, 6. Pfann agrees, "The Improper Application of Statistics in `The Lost Tomb of Jesus,' " 1-2.

47. Zias, "Deconstructing the Second and Hopefully Last Coming of Simcha and the BAR Crowd," 2.

48. Witherington, "The Jesus Tomb? 'Titanic' Talpiot Tomb Theory Sunk from the Start,", 4.

49. Tabor, The Jesus Dynasty, 26; repeated on 27.

50. Quoted by Christopher Mims, "Says Scholar Whose Work Was Used in the Upcoming Jesus Tomb Documentary: 'I think it's completely mishandled. I am angry.' " Scientific American.com, March 2, 2007, 3. Zias concurs in this evaluation regarding the DNA testing (Zias, "Deconstructing the Second and Hopefully Last Coming of Simcha and the BAR Crowd," March 7, 2007, 2).

STATISTICAL ARGUMENT, OTHER PROBLEMS, AND CONCLUSIONS

In the last chapter we argued that the Talpiot Hypothesis falls substantially short on the issues of the incidence of family names, the identification of the Mariamene ossuary as that of Mary Magdalene, the identification of the tenth ossuary as that of James the brother of Jesus, and the DNA testing.

Our chief subject in this chapter is to evaluate the statistical argument provided by those who support the Talpiot thesis, which they think shows to a high degree of likelihood (600:1) that the Talpiot Tomb is the actual burial site of Jesus' family. Several other problems with the overall thesis also need to be mentioned, some of which are rarely discussed. Then we will view a number of scholarly conclusions to the Talpiot Hypothesis.

Statistical Confirmation?

Statistics are based on the information provided; adjustments to that information translate into huge changes in the numbers

- Mark Goodacre thinks that "The major part of the case that the Talpiot Tomb is Jesus' family tomb is based on the statistical claim."[1] If so, then this may be the most crucial portion of our discussion.

- The statistician used in formulating the Talpiot Hypothesis, Andrey Feuerverger of the University of Toronto, has said often that his "computations depend heavily on the assumptions that go into it." This is incredibly crucial, as he acknowledges: "Should even one of these assumptions not be satisfied then the results will not be statistically meaningful." For example, the identification of Mariamene with Mary Magdalene "drives the outcome of the computations substantially."[2] Similarly, Feuerverger reportedly told Ted Koppel: "I must work from the interpretations given to me, and the strength of the calculations are based on those assumptions." For example, regarding the Mariamene ossuary, "if for some reason one were to read it as just a regular form of the name Maria, in that case the calculation produced is not as impressive, and the statistical significance would wash out considerably."[3]

DATA AND CORRECT ASSMPTIONS

STATISTICAL CALCULATION

ACCURATE RESULTS

DATA AND INCORRECT ASSMPTIONS

STATISTICAL CALCULATION

INACCURATE RESULTS

✠ Accordingly, Feuerverger now realizes that statistics cannot conclude whether or not the Talpiot family is that of Jesus of Nazareth. He states, "It is not in the purview of statistics to conclude whether or not this tombsite is that of the New Testament family." The reason for this is because, "Any such conclusion much more rightfully belongs to the purview of biblical historical scholars who are in a much better position to assess the assumptions entering into such computations." He concludes the matter: "I now believe that I should not assert any conclusions connecting this tomb with any hypothetical one of the NT family."[4] This indicates the ultimate importance of investigating these Talpiot Tomb assumptions. Since the assumptions feed the statistics, we must be sure that they are based on correct data.

✠ Mathematician Joe D'Mello pointed out several problems with Feuerverger's computations, and made key clarifications about what is being claimed. In particular, his chief point seems to be that slight changes in the interpretations or factual basis very quickly change the overall conclusions.[5]

✠ Joseph Fitzmeyer is typical of many when he argues that the Talpiot Hypothesis contains far too "iffy" conditionals which basically all must be true in order to arrive at their conclusions. Further, too many rhetorical questions are meant to be answered positively, when a negative answer will change the end result. As he concludes regarding this thesis: "Speculation is rife . . . ."[6]

> "I MUST WORK FROM THE INTERPRETATIONS GIVEN TO ME, AND THE STRENGTH OF THE CALCULATIONS ARE BASED ON THOSE ASSUMPTIONS."
>
> ...ANDREY FEUERVERGER

Some Questionable Assumptions: General Issues

✠ Virtually all scholars who have responded to the issues agree that the assumptions passed on to Feuerverger must be questioned very seriously, as can be seen below. Goodacre calls these assumptions a "fatal bias" that plagues the analysis from the beginning.[7]

✠ Scholars have isolated several of the Talpiot Hypothesis assumptions that they think need to be challenged. We will begin with four general concerns regarding the computed frequency of names, the number of persons who were often buried in the same ossuaries, the extended family nature of these rock tombs, and the several generations who buried their loved ones there. If these are not properly accounted for, as they apparently were not, then the statistics will be seriously slanted.

✠ As Tabor is very careful to point out, the first

round of computations had nothing to do with the actual family of Jesus of Nazareth, but simply asked the frequency of these six or seven persons being altogether in the same family grouping.[8] We will dispute momentarily whether all these names existed as a single family under one roof, which it now seems that they assuredly did not. But here we will simply point out that the odds of any group of six or seven people being together would be very improbable.

For example, what are the odds that a particular grouping of six or seven people were at my house last night watching a football game? Like the names in the Talpiot Tomb, most of these friends could have names that are among the most common in our society, but a couple of them could go by nicknames and one could include a "son of" designation. What are the odds that precisely these six or seven people and no others would be at my home, particularly if two or three of them have fairly distinctive names? We should also expect very high odds.

So it would appear that the first round of the computation shows virtually nothing except that these half dozen or so people would not normally be all together at once! This is especially the case when a very similar cluster of Jewish names, including Mary, Martha, Matthew, Joseph, and Jesus, have been reported from a tomb on the Mount of Olives, as mentioned in the last chapter.[9] Apparently the Talpiot cluster of names is not so rare as supposed.

※ Stephen Pfann says that the 600:1 probability that the Talpiot Tomb belonged to Jesus' family "is based upon a number of fallacies and a general misuse of statistics." To identify the

The "Caiaphas Ossuary." Caiaphas was the name of the chief priest at the time of Jesus' crucifixion. This ossuary was found near Jerusalem in 1990 and contained the bones of several people. Photo: David Rubinger//Time Life Pictures/Getty Images.

family as being that of Jesus of Nazareth is "pure speculation." Most importantly, individual ossuaries "often contained the remains of more than one individual" (for example, the Caiphas ossuary held the remains of several people).[10] In the last chapter we already recounted Zias' published results of a Jewish tomb where 15 ossuaries contained the remains of 88 different people! Accordingly, Zias thinks that the Talpiot Hypothesis statistics were "rigged."[11] That multiple persons were buried specifically in the Talpiot ossuaries seems to be more than clear. Kloner estimated that 17 individuals were buried in the ten ossuaries![12]

Further, as noted by Rollston, rock tombs held the remains of extended families, including one's uncles, aunts, cousins, and grandparents.[13] Witherington argues that we know that unrelated Christians were often buried together, so it is not necessary that all of the ossuaries from a particular site even be from just a single family.[14] After all, Matthew claims that Jesus was buried in a tomb belonging to Joseph of Arimathea (Matt. 27:60), and the clear intent of all four Gospels is that Jesus was not interred in his own family tomb! Moreover, perhaps most crucially, Zias reminds us that these Jewish tombs usually held four to five generations of extended family members, and that is why stats "simply cannot be computed."[15] Witherington argues that the three languages found on the ossuaries in the Talpiot tomb indicate that it was probably multi-generational.[16] We might add that that the large number of persons inside the Talpiot Tomb (35 people according to Kloner but only a third or so of that according to Tabor[17]) is another indication that this tomb held far more than a single generational family. Most damaging of all, Kloner reported in his 1996 report that this was also so in the Talpiot Tomb: "This burial cave was probably used for three or four generations."[18]

That Tabor plainly wants to argue otherwise on these points[19] seems to be an indication of his realization that if the Talpiot Tomb indeed did contain the remains of several people in the individual ossuaries, plus an extended family of persons, and over a few or even several generations, then this counts very heavily against his argument that the named ossuaries had to contain people who were directly related to each other, practically under one roof. If they were not directly related, originating in the same household, then the probabilities of finding "the Jesus family" almost disappear. So on these three general points there is much to be lost from the Talpiot Hypothesis, as we will see.

More Questionable Assumptions: Specific Issues

✖ Besides these general concerns, scholars have also demarcated several more specific Talpiot Hypothesis assumptions that they think are quite faulty. There is a remarkable amount of scholarly agreement here with regard to which theses are the most questionable. We will especially mention the assumptions regarding Mariamene, Jose, Matthew, Judah, and Jesus. Along with Mary and except for Judah, these are the individual persons who make up the Talpiot statistics.

The Mariamene ossuary. Photo: Mariana Salzberger, Courtesy of Israel Antiquities Authority via Getty Images.

✖ With Mariamene there are at least two main issues: Was she the same person as Mary Magdalene? Was she married to Jesus?

- We argued in the last chapter that there is very little chance that Mariamene was Mary Magdalene, and we won't repeat those arguments here. There is nothing that could really be called historical (or other) evidence for this identification. The suggested sources are not only very late, far after the time of Jesus, they are not even clear that Mary Magdalene is this same individual. This is why Pfann says that the chief source "should be considered irrelevant to the discussion, being three centuries too late for consideration."[20]

• Was Mariamene married to the Jesus in the Talpiot Tomb? Ted Koppel asked Carney Matheson, who performed the tests, about the conclusion that DNA revealed that Jesus and Mariamene were probably married. Matheson replied: "There is a statement in the film that has been taken out of context. While marriage is a possibility, other relationships like father and daughter, paternal cousins, sister-in-law, or indeed two unrelated individuals [are also possible] . . . . My conclusion is that they are not maternally related. You cannot genetically test for marriage."[21]

JESUS ← MARRIED / PATERNAL COUSINS / IN-LAWS / FATHER/DAUGHTER / UNRELATED → **MARIAMENE**

• Goodacre concludes the matter as far as the vast majority of scholars are concerned: "Now given that no reputable historian of Christian origins seriously thinks that Jesus was married to Mary Magdalene (or anyone else, as far as we know), the presence of a Mariamene in the tomb can in no way be allowed to be a part of the statistical calculations here."[22]

Was Jose the brother of the Jesus buried in the Talpiot Tomb? Since we already have one Joseph in the tomb (Jesus' father), it is a far simpler view to hold that Jose is the familial nickname (perhaps given by his wife or other family members) for this same person, rather than to suppose a second person of the same name.[23] Further, there is also some archaeological evidence for this view, as well. L.Y. Rahmani, in the standard scholarly work on Jewish ossuaries that was used by Jacobovici and Pellegrino, said that, "The similarity of this [Jose] ossuary and its inscription with that of Marya on No. 706, both from the same tomb, may indicate that these are the ossuaries of the parents of Yeshua (No. 704) and the grandparents of Yehuda (No. 702)."[24] But it seems that the only major reason to overlook Rahmani's sensible suggestion is that to claim that it is Jesus' of Nazareth's brother fits far better with the Talpiot Hypothesis.

Inscription on the Matthew ossuary. Photo: Uriel Sinai/Getty Images.

Initially, Jacobovici and Pellegrino thought that Matthew would be close to the family of Jesus of Nazareth because the name appears more than once in Luke's geneology.[25] But to their credit, Feuerverger left it out of the second computation because the name is not explicitly mentioned in the Gospels as a family member.[26] Thus, although it did not figure in the statistical computation, most scholars thought that the Matthew ossuary shouldn't have entered the discussion at all, except as a negative factor (see below).

✄ Judah the son of Jesus also did not figure as part of Feuerverger's statistics. Not only did most scholars reject the notion that this could be the son of Jesus, but as with Matthew, many scholars still wanted to make Judah's presence in the tomb a negative factor (also see below).

Inscription on the Jesus ossuary. Photo: Mariana Salzberger, Courtesy of Israel Antiquities Authority via Getty Images..

✄ What about the ossuary of the Talpiot man named "Jesus son of Joseph"? How rare is such a name? A few considerations are behind the reason why the ossuary name was virtually ignored by the Jewish scholars who worked on the Talpiot Tomb find.

- There is at least one other ossuary with this designation and Kloner noted that there were three or four such ossuaries.[27]
- Using available listings of first-century names, estimates indicate that, during the time the ossuaries were used, Jerusalem would contain approximately 1008 men named Jesus, who also had a father named Joseph![28] Intriguingly, Pellegrino uses these same figures, including 7,200 men in Jerusalem named Jesus, 1008 of

whom would have a Joseph for a father.[29] But Ingermanson points out a mathematical error in Pellegrino's figures, dropping his final figures from 2.5 million:1 all the way down to 31:1.[30] But as we will see, even this reduced figure is far too high.

I think that we also need to add to this number, in order to allow for other Jewish males with the same names from outside the city who could have, for whatever reason, been buried in Jerusalem. After all, Jesus was from Galilee and the Talpiot Hypothesis still places his tomb in this city. But it would seem that this large number of men who were also named "Jesus son of Joseph" would change significantly the Talpiot statistics, as we will see below.

✠ Many (if not most) researchers, however, think that there is more than these numbers alone. There are also important factors present here which should compute *negatively* against the computations that the Talpiot Tomb family is the same as Jesus of Nazareth's family. Ingermanson calls this the "not-Jesus factor."[31]

✠ Even Jacobovici and Pellegrino are well aware of this. They point out that if other names were present in the Talpiot Tomb, such as Jonah or Daniel, this "would have led us to question the entire assemblage" because these names would not fit in Jesus of Nazareth's family.[32] Feuerverger, too, acknowledges this factor, stating that there are no other "negatives" beyond those names that we already know from the tomb "that would in and of themselves invalidate 'the hypothesis' or that would appear to lessen its likelihood."[33]

✳ The difference, however, is that while Jacobovici, Pellegrino, and Feuerverger acknowledge this possibility, many scholars hold that there are *several "not-Jesus" factors that detract from the Talpiot statistics.* For example, Goodacre thinks that this is simply crucial to the equation, since "non-matches" with Jesus of Nazareth "contradict the literary record."

> "COLLECTIVELY THESE POINTS ARE DEVASTATING, SINCE THE STATISTICAL ANALYSES PRESENTED IN THE FILM ARE BASED ON CERTAIN ASSUMPTIONS MADE ABOUT THESE NAMES."
>
> JODI MAGNESS

✳ When these negatives are ignored or treated as neutral, we have an "essential problem" and that is why the Talpiot case is "severely flawed."[34] Some of the problems have been alluded to immediately above. Here are the main ones, noted by many scholars[35]:

✳ **There is no early historical evidence that Jesus had a son.** To invent such a person ("Judah" or whomever) and read the data that way is illegitimate. True, the Talpiot Hypothesis, as we have just pointed out above, does not include Judah in its statistical computations. But that is the point: they thought that it was not a *positive* finding that related to their conclusion. But many scholars think that this is one of the facts that show that the Talpiot Tomb is *not* that of Jesus' family. In my opinion, Ingermanson places far too high the suggested chances against Jesus having a son.[36] But the "Judah factor" still militates against this being Jesus of Nazareth.

❈ **We could say almost the same thing about Matthew.** He does not fit the Jesus family. And again, we have already said that Matthew was not counted in the second Talpiot computation, but it's worse than that. For this is another factor that, while possible, actually detracts from the Jesus of Nazareth supposition. As Witherington states, the Matthew reference is a liability, because even though "Ancestors are irrelevant . . . . It's as simple as this: this is a family tomb and none of Jesus' brothers are Matthew."[37] Tabor objects to Judah being a negative factor, but only says that "if" such a son existed, this might help in some unexplained ways, without commenting further.[38]

❈ Probably the case that bothers scholars the most is the **comparison between Mariamene and Mary Magdalene,** because the case is so flimsy and is opposed by all of the early historical data. Not only must she be taken out of the Talpiot computations, where she plays a very major role, but this, too, is seen as another negative factor that also detracts from the case that this may be Jesus of Nazareth.

❈ Scholars conclude that this "not-Jesus factor" is very significant. Magness sums up: "Taken individually, each of these points weakens the case for the identification of the Talpiot tomb as the tomb of Jesus and his family. Collectively these points are devastating, since the statistical analyses presented in the film are based on certain assumptions made about these names."[39] Goodacre also summarizes the matter: "the greater the number of non-matches, the less impressive the cluster becomes. Or, to put it another way, it stops being a cluster of striking names when the cluster is diluted with non-matches."

✂ Playing creatively on Jacobovici's use of the Beatles analogy and the significance of the name "Ringo,"[10] Goodacre illustrates the problem: "What we actually have is the equivalence of a tomb with the names John, Paul, George, Martin, Alan and Ziggy." Regarding the misuse of Mariamene, Matthew, and Judah, Goodacre concludes: "All data must be included. *You cannot cherry pick or manipulate your data before doing your statistical analysis.*"[41]

NOT-JESUS FACTORS

JUDAH, SON OF JESUS	NO HISTORICAL EVIDENCE JESUS HAD A SON
MATTHEW	THE LIST OF JESUS' BROTHERS DOES NOT INCLUDE A MATTHEW
MARIAMENE AND MARY MAGDALENE	NO HISTORICAL REASONS TO CONNECT MARIAMENE AND MARY MAGDALENE
NAME CLUSTER	NOT ALL DATA INCLUDED

* ANY ONE OF THESE POINTS DAMAGES THE TALPIOT HYPOTHESIS, BUT TAKEN TOGETHER THEY DEVASTATE IT SINCE THE STATISTICAL COMPUTATIONS ARE BASED ON THE ASSUMPTIONS THESE POINTS MILITATE AGAINST.

What Do the Reworked Statistics Look Like?

✂ There is *strikingly little* that we can know from the Talpiot Tomb with regard to direct, blood relations between the family members there. Two of the most crucial things to keep in mind about the nature of these Jewish burial tombs are that they were used for extended families, and that these families were buried there for three to five generations.

Assuming that the first name on the "son of Joseph" ossuary is indeed "Jesus" and that there was only one man buried in the tomb with the name of Jesus (unlike the two Marys), all we can know is that Joseph, Jesus, and Judah are related as father, son, and grandson, respectively. We cannot even know that one of the Marys is one of their mothers, or what relation Jose or Matthew were to the rest of the family. The others could be grandparents, cousins, aunts, uncles, adopted children, step-parents, previous children of the step-parents, or the spouses of many of these persons![42] Or the other names in the tomb could be people who all lived and died in this extended family, but during a earlier generation, perhaps before the Talpiot Jesus was even born!

So we cannot state any known conclusions concerning Maria, Mariamene, Jose, or Matthew. Thus, quite contrary to the second computation of the Talpiot Hypothesis "Statistics Overview," we cannot use figures for Mariamene, Maria, or Jose. We simply do not know that information.

INCOMPATIBLE CLAIMS MADE BY THE TALPIOT ADVOCATES

600:1
IN FAVOR
WITHOUT
"NOT-JESUS" FACTORS

IN SPITE OF

1008:1
JERUSALEM MEN NAMED
JESUS, SON OF JOSEPH

�֍ We just said that even Pellegrino (and apparently Jacobovici, too) acknowledges that the chances of a man named Jesus who also had a father named Joseph who lived in Jerusalem during the era of the ossuaries is 1 in 79 and that approximately 1008 Jewish men probably had that relationship. Just "straight up," even after conceding the items mentioned above, that is still a 1008:1 chance against the Talpiot Tomb being the tomb of Jesus. Need we go any further on these grounds alone?

But unfortunately for the Talpiot Hypothesis, to compute for the name Judah takes us away from the known family of Jesus of Nazareth. In fact, from what we know historically, if the Talpiot Jesus had a son named Judah, that would be more than enough to argue that he is indeed one of the 1008 other men in Jerusalem who were named Jesus with a father named Joseph. For if we gave Jesus a 20 percent chance of having a son, which is probably a much higher percentage than most would grant, this alone would change the probability to 5000:1 that it is not Jesus of Nazareth!

Probably no one has done more work on the statistics of the Talpiot Tomb than Randy Ingermanson. In his initial essay on the topic, he concluded that there was a 10,000:1 chance that the Talpiot Tomb Jesus is not Jesus of Nazareth.[43] (After his study, Rosebrough concluded that there was a 15,000:1 chance against all the major premises of the Talpiot Hypothesis being true, from which Rosebrough derived the title of his essay, "archaeological identity theft"![44])

But Ingermanson went much further with a second study. Teaming up with Jay Cost, they used a very sophisticated application of Bayes' Theorem, a highly recognized means of using calculus in "improving an initial probability estimate in light of new information." They figured the problem in several ways, depending on how people answer the "fuzzy factors" where there are differences of opinion. For a typical historian, they arrived at a

19,000:1 chance against the Talpiot Tomb being that of Jesus. For a historian who leans toward this being Jesus' tomb, the chances are estimated at 1,100:1. For the historian who leans toward it not being Jesus' tomb, the odds drop all the way to 5,000,000:1!

Basically, the lesson of their study is that there are not enough realistic "fuzzy factors" to turn the odds in favor of the Talpiot Tomb being Jesus' burial place.[45] As Ingermanson concludes, "The article shows 5 different test cases that give estimates that would be computed by people with a wide range of different mindsets. The interesting thing is that, despite vast differences in assumptions, the final results are not terribly different."[46] Overall, their conclusions are absolutely devastating to the Talpiot Hypothesis.[47]

TALPIOT ODDS AND BAYES' THEOREM

19,000:1 AGAINST	**1,100:1** AGAINST	**5,000,000:1** AGAINST
TYPICAL OPINION OF FUZZY FACTORS	SYMPATHETIC OPINION OF FUZZY FACTORS	UNSYMPATHETIC OPINION OF FUZZY FACTORS

Additional Problems

In the many critiques of the Talpiot Hypothesis, there are a number of additional issues that ought to be mentioned. These tend to be somewhat less substantial, and a couple simply raise questions, but they still should be considered in any treatment of the subject.

Are there dating problems? Kloner wrote in his original article that the Talpiot Tomb could be dated from the end of the First Century BCE until 70 CE.[48] Of course, if the date is actually prior to about 30, this entire discussion is moot. On the other hand, Witherington argues for a post-70 date for the tomb, which is still possible because it is known that Jewish osslegium, or ossuary reburial, continued past 70 at least until 125, into the time of Bar Kokhba. Witherington finds potential indications of this conclusion in the following: 1) the tomb is not located in Old Jerusalem; 2) the three languages and especially because early Christians usually did not speak Greek; 3) the ornamental marking outside the tomb "is meant to attract attention and draw people to the tomb," which is arguably the opposite of pre-70 times when Christians were "beleaguered" let alone trying to show off where Jesus was buried![49]

※ Many scholars have mentioned that if Jesus' family had a family tomb, it would most likely be located in Nazareth, not Jerusalem.[50] For example, Alan Segal asks, "Why would Jesus' family have a tomb outside of Jerusalem if they were from Nazareth?"[51] Magness cites Rahmani's research, and indicates that the custom was for Judean families to indicate ancestry by mentioning the father. "But in rock-cut tombs owned by non-Judean families . . . it was customary to indicate the deceased's place of origin" instead. At the very least, Magness notes that "we could expect that at least some of the ossuary inscriptions to reflect their Galilean origins . . . ." Further, if Jesus' family had owned their own tomb, Joseph would never have had to intervene.[52]

※ Likewise, some of these same scholars have added the point that Jesus' family was not wealthy and stone tombs are very expensive.[53] But Tabor countered with the strong protest that wealthy followers of Jesus such as Joseph of Arimathea or Lazarus (who also had a rock tomb) could have paid for the Jesus family tomb, just as Joseph did with his first burial, because of their "extraordinary devotion" to him.[54]

※ Zias seemed incensed by the Talpiot Hypothesis interpretation of the symbols on the tomb. For example, the mysterious "X" marking on ossuaries are not Christian symbols, but simply an indication of which way the lid fits—it will not work in the reverse! Zias concludes, "Duh . . . ."[55]

- Jesus not called son of Joseph by any one who knew him intimately—neither by family members nor by his disciples.[56]

- Although it would not necessarily refute any of the data, more than one scholar mentioned what they considered the problem is that the Talpiot Tomb claim was first voiced by the popular media instead of having the appeal made in the peer-reviewed literature. For example, Jodi Magness makes this point.[57]

Statistical studies fail to support the conclusion that the Talpiot Tomb is the burial place of Jesus of Nazareth. Once again, every claim has been countered by many devastating critical responses. Scarcely has a thesis regarding the historical Jesus faced such a scholarly pummeling, especially considering that the complaints have issued from those of various theological persuasions across the spectrum.

It is sufficient here to recall that both sides even acknowledge that there were more than a thousand Jewish men in Jerusalem alone during the time of ossuary burials who were named "Jesus," and whose father was also named "Joseph." The auxiliary claims, along with several other problems, only move us further away from the initial hypothesis. As Ingermanson has graphically argued above, the case against the Talpiot Hypothesis is so decisive that it is almost a moot point how one answers the relevant questions. The conclusion is still the same: this is not the tomb of Jesus of Nazareth.

Notes

1. Mark Goodacre, "The Statistical Case for the Identity of the `Jesus Family Tomb,' " NT Gateway Weblog, March 1, 2007, 1 (http://ntgateway.com/weblog/2007/03/statistical-case-for-identity-of-jesus-.html, downloaded on March 6, 2007).

2. Andrey Feuerverger, "Dear Statistical Colleagues," March 12, 2007, the quotations appear on pp. 1, 2 (posted at: http://fisher.ustat.toronto.edu/andrey/OfficeHrs.txt and downloaded on March 23, 2007.

3. Discovery Channel Interview with Ted Koppel, "The Lost Tomb of Jesus: A Critical Look," March 4, 2007).

4. Andrey Feuerverger, "Dear Statistical Colleagues," 1.

5. Joe D'Mello, "The Correct Interpretation of Dr. Andrey Feuerverger's 1:600 Odds Calculation," NT Gateway Weblog, March 2, 2007, 1-5.

6. Joseph Fitzmyer, book review of Simcha Jacobovici and Charles Pellegrino, *The Jesus Family Tomb in America: The National Catholic Weekly*, date?, 3. (http:/www.americamagazine.org/BookReview.cfm?articleTypeID=31&textID=5404&issue, downloaded on April 2, 2007).

7. Goodacre, "The Statistical Case for the Identity of the 'Jesus Family Tomb,' NT Gateway, 2.

8. James Tabor, email to select colleagues and friends, February 28, 2007, 2-3.

9. "Dominus Flevit," 2 (downloaded on March 22, 2007); email from Michael S. Heiser, March 13, 2007.

10. Stephen Pfann, "The Improper Application of Statistics in 'The Lost Tomb of Jesus,' " University of the Holy Land, 2007, 1-2. Pfann also argues the following issues: most ancient Jewish tombs have already been looted, not all ossuaries have been saved even after discovered, and Rahmani notes that only about 25 percent of ossuaries have names on them.

11. Joe Zias, "Deconstructing the Second and Hopefully Last Coming of Simcha and the BAR Crowd," March 7, 2007, 2-3.

12. Amos Kloner, "A Tomb with Inscribed Ossuaries in East Talpiot, Jerusalem," `Antiqot, Vol 29 (1996), 22.

13. Christopher A. Rollston, "Prosopography and the Talpiyot Yeshua Family Tomb: Pensees of a

Paleographer," Society of Biblical Liturature Forum, March 13, 2007, 3-4.

14. Witherington, "Problems Multiply for Jesus Tomb Theory," February 28, 2007, 5.

15. Zias, "Deconstructing the Second and Hopefully Last Coming of Simcha and the BAR Crowd," 2.

16. Witherington, "Problems Multiply for Jesus Tomb Theory," 1.

17. See this discussion in the last chapter.

18. Kloner, "A Tomb with Inscribed Ossuaries in East Talpiyot, Jerusalem," 21.

19. James Tabor, "The Talpiot Tomb: An Overview," The Jesus Dynasty Blog, March 24, 2007, 2-3.

20. Pfann, "The Improper Application of Statistics in 'The Lost Tomb of Jesus,' " 3. For some of the scholars who agree that Mariamene is not Mary Magdalene, see Jodi Magness, "Has the Tomb of Jesus Been Discovered?" in Society of Biblical Literature Forum, March, 2007, 4; Rollston, "Prosopography and the Talpiyot Yeshua Family Tomb: Pensees of a Paleographer," 3-4; Goodacre, "The Statistical Case for the Identity of the "Jesus Family Tomb," 1, 3; Michael Barber, "7 Reasons Cameron's Theory is Sinking," February 27, 2007, 4; Chris Rosebrough, "Archaeological Identity Theft: The Lost Tomb of Jesus Fails to Make the Grade," Extreme Theology, 2-3;

21. Discovery Channel Interview with Ted Koppel, "The Lost Tomb of Jesus: A Critical Look," March 4, 2007.

22. Goodacre, "The Statistical Case for the Identity of the "Jesus Family Tomb," 1.

23. Rollston, "Prosopography and the Talpiyot Yeshua Family Tomb: Pensees of a Paleographer," p. 4; Rosebrough, "Archaeological Identity Theft: The Lost Tomb of Jesus Fails to Make the Grade," 4.

24. L.Y. Rahmani, A Catalog of Jewish Ossuaries in the Collections of the State of Israel (Jerusalem: Israel Antiquities and Israel Academy of Sciences and Humanities, 1994), No. 705.

25. Simcha Jacobovici and Charles Pellegrino, The Jesus Family Tomb (N.Y.: Harper Collins, 2007), 78.

26. "Statistics Overview" from Andrey Feuerverger's analysis, Discovery Channel Website.

27. David Horovitz, Question and Answer interview with Amos Kloner: "Kloner: A Great Story, but Nonsense," Jerusalem Post, February 27, 2007, 1; Ben Witherington, "The Jesus Tomb Show—Biblical Archaeologists Reject Discovery Channel Show's Claims," March 5, 2007, 4.

28. Randy Ingermanson, "Statistics and the 'Jesus Family Tomb,' " March 3, 2007, 2-3 (available at http://www.ingermanson.com/jesus/art/stats.php, downloaded on March 13, 2007).

29. Jacobovici and Pellegrino, The Jesus Family Tomb, 75; also 77.

30. Cf. Ingermanson, "Statistics and the 'Jesus Family Tomb,'" 8 with Jacobovici and Pellegrino, The Jesus Family Tomb, 82.

31. Ingermanson, "Statistics and the 'Jesus Family Tomb,'" 9.

32. Jacobovici and Pellegrino, The Jesus Family Tomb, 78.

33. Andrey Feuerverger, "Dear Statistical Colleagues," 3.

34. Goodacre, "The Statistical Case for the Identity of the 'Jesus Family Tomb,'" 1.

35. Examples include Magness, "Has the Tomb of Jesus Been Discovered?" 4; Goodacre, "The Statistical Case for the Identity of the 'Jesus Family Tomb,'" 1; Witherington, "The Jesus Tomb? 'Titanic' Talpiot Tomb Theory Sunk from the Start," 4; Ingermanson, "Statistics and the 'Jesus Family Tomb,'" 6, 9; Rosebrough, "Archaeological Identity Theft: The Lost Tomb of Jesus Fails to Make the Grade," especially 2; Barber, "7 Reasons Cameron's Theory is Sinking," 1-2; cf. Rollston, "Prosopography and the Talpiyot Yeshua Family Tomb: Pensees of a Paleographer," 3.

36. Ingermanson, "Statistics and the 'Jesus Family Tomb,'" 6.

37. Witherington, "Problems Multiply for Jesus Tomb Theory," 1-2.

38. Tabor, "The Talpiot Tomb: An Overview," 3.

39. Magness, "Has the Tomb of Jesus been Discovered?" 4.

40. Simcha Jacobovici, "Probability," found at: http://www.jesusfamilytomb.com/evidence/probability.html (downloaded on April 8, 2007).

41. Emphasis by Goodacre in, "The Statistical Case for the Identity of the "Jesus Family Tomb," 3.

42. See especially Rollston, "Prosopography and the Talpiyot

Yeshua Family Tomb: Pensees of a Paleographer," 3.

43. Ingermanson, "Statistics and the `Jesus Family Tomb,'" 6, 10.

44. Rosebrough, "Archaeological Identity Theft: The Lost Tomb of Jesus Fails to Make the Grade," 4, 6.

45. Randy Ingermanson and Jay Cost, "Bayes' Theorem and the 'Jesus Family Tomb,' " March 25, 2007.

46. Personal email from Randy Ingermanson, March 26, 2007.

47. Incredibly, in the article "Bayes' Theorem and the `Jesus Family Tomb,' " Ingermanson and Cost provide an Excel spreadsheet where interested readers can answer the same "fuzzy factors" and create their own odds!

48. Kloner, "A Tomb with Inscribed Ossuaries in East Talpiyot, Jerusalem," 21.

49. Witherington, "Problems Multiply for Jesus Tomb Theory," 1, 4-5.

50. Magness as quoted in Christopher Mims, "Special Report: Has James Cameron Found Jesus's Tomb or Is It Just a Statistical Error?" Scientific American, March 2, 2007, 3; Witherington, "The Jesus Tomb? 'Titanic' Talpiot Tomb Theory Sunk from the Start," 4; Michael Licona, "First Person: Has the Family Tomb of Jesus been Found?" BP News, February 27, 2007, 1).

51. Alan Segal as quoted in Lisa Miller and Joanna Chen, "The Tomb of Jesus Christ?" Newsweek, March 5, 2007, 3.

52. Magness, "Has the Tomb of Jesus been Discovered?" 3-4.

53. Segal as quoted by Lisa Miller and Joanna Chen, "The Tomb of Jesus Christ?" 3; Magness as quoted in Mims, "Special Report: Has James Cameron Found Jesus's Tomb or Is It Just a Statistical Error?" 3; Licona, "First Person: Has the Family Tomb of Jesus been Found?" 1.

54. James D. Tabor, "Two Burials of Jesus of Nazareth and the Talpiot Yeshua Tomb," Society of Biblical Literature Forum, March, 2007, 2.

55. Zias, "Deconstructing the Second and Hopefully Last Coming of Simcha and the BAR Crowd," 3.

56. Witherington, "Problems Multiply for Jesus Tomb Theory," 2.

57. Magness, "Has the Tomb of Jesus been Discovered?" 1.

THE RESURRECTION OF JESUS

Now we reach the last chapter of the Talpiot Tomb saga. Given the claims of those who think that this is the family tomb of Jesus of Nazareth, how can we account for what history says happened on the first Easter? Answering this question is one of the most difficult for those who support the Talpiot thesis.

From the beginning, we need to be very clear when we address this topic with regard to our use of the New Testament and other ancient documents. We must emphasize that the argument definitely does not assume that the Talpiot Hypothesis must be mistaken just because it disagrees with the Bible, or with Christian tradition, or with Christian beliefs. Unless there are firm reasons for believing these sources, this would be to reject the thesis for the wrong reasons.

Thus we will take a different approach. Almost exclusively, we will make use only of the established historical information that is generally accepted by the vast majority of scholars who study this topic. More crucially, when scholars agree about particular historical data, it is almost always because there are strong reasons for believing this information. This is especially the case when the specialists who agree about these facts disagree concerning what they do with the rest of Christian belief. While I will not be able to argue here how this historical basis is established, I have done so elsewhere in great detail.[1]

In other words, the responses that represent the most difficulty for the Talpiot claims are those that are drawn from accredited information that is approved by scholars precisely because they have strong reasons for doing so. Therefore, if these historical facts make it very difficult to accept the Talpiot Hypothesis, then this will be a strong hurdle for the thesis to overcome. It will require the advocates to disprove the widespread scholarly basis behind the objections.

The Empty Tomb of Jesus

In all our ancient sources, friends and foes alike acknowledged that the tomb in which Jesus was buried was found empty shortly afterwards.

Our earliest source (1 Cor. 15:4) states that the discovery of the vacated tomb of Jesus occurred just three days after the crucifixion. All four Gospels report that the women who visited Jesus' tomb discovered that it was open and empty. And it was reported that even the Jewish authorities thought that the tomb was empty.[2]

Why should anyone believe that this is actually what happened? Perhaps surprisingly, scholars have provided more than twenty reasons for the historicity of the empty tomb. The most frequently mentioned is the unanimous agreement that women were the first witnesses. In the patriarchal culture of first-century AD Palestine, women were unlikely to be asked to give important testimony. Generally, there was an inverse relationship between the importance of a particular subject and whether or not a woman would be allowed to testify in court.

Given this scenario, why are the women listed by all our sources as the first witnesses to the empty tomb, unless it is true? Even further, why would we be told that the male disciples reacted by belittling the women and accusing them of spreading tales—basically gossip (see Luke 24:11)? These are examples of what scholars call the principle of embarrassment—that it is unlikely that authors will embarrass their heroes without very good reasons. But the texts clearly report these embarrassing accounts.

On the other hand, if you want to document something as important as the empty tomb, and you are as free with your sources as some scholars think, why not simply make up a story that says that the men found the empty tomb, so that their testimony would more readily be received? And even if you use the women, certainly do not make the future leaders of the church, the male disciples, criticize the women! That would mean that those who took

Jesus' place were badly mistaken. But the church needs to trust the disciples for their wise counsel!

This is all backward and a horrible way to establish your case—that is, unless it is precisely what happened! These are some of the reasons why scholars take so seriously the "embarrassing" female testimony concerning finding the vacated tomb.

Another reason to accept the empty tomb is that the city of Jerusalem should have been the very last place chosen for such a report if it were not so. Why? Because the city was both the birthplace of the church and home to many enemies who opposed the message. An afternoon walk to the tomb by either friend or foe could either verify or debunk the claim. If the tomb were not empty, how easily could the claim have been disproven?

Some will object that the story of the women visiting the tomb does not surface until the Gospel of Mark, about 35 or 40 years after the events. But we must not miss something important here. The predominant view of afterlife among the Jews of this day is clearly that of bodily resurrection.[3] So how could the disciples have gotten away with proclaiming that Jesus had risen and appeared to them after his death if the stone still remained in front of his tomb? That story would have found credence only if the stone was moved and the tomb was empty.

We will just mention one more argument for the empty tomb. Ancient historian Paul Maier reminds us of a common standard in the field: "Many facts from antiquity rest on just one ancient source, while two or three sources in agreement generally render the fact unimpeachable."[4] But the empty tomb is attested by between three and six independent sources, both in the Gospels and elsewhere.[5] This is simply excellent evidence by ancient standards.

So for these and many other reasons, that Jesus' burial tomb was empty very shortly after his death on the cross is the best explanation for the data. How does the Talpiot Hypothesis explain this data?

The Talpiot Tomb versus Jesus' Traditional Burial and Empty Tomb

According to the Talpiot Hypothesis, Jesus of Nazareth died by crucifixion and was buried initially in a tomb, for perhaps a year, waiting for his flesh to rot. Then later, his bones would have been reburied in the Talpiot family tomb, in the ossuary that bears his name.

BURIAL AND TOMB DATA

BIBLICAL ACCOUNT	TALPIOT HYPOTHESIS
MULTIPLE ATTESTATION (3-6 EARLY SOURCES)	NO ANCIENT SOURCES
PRINCIPLE OF EMBARASSMENT (FEMALE TESTIMONY)	CONTRARY TO EARLIEST SOURCES
JERUSALEM LOCATION EASILY VERIFIED	CLUSTER OF BILICAL NAMES
	YESHUA OSSUARY
	SPECULATION

TOMB DISCOVERD EMPTY ON THIRD DAY

BONES PLACED IN OSSUARY AND MOVED TO TALPIOT TOMB

According to James Tabor, a likely scenario would involve Jesus' original but temporary burial in a private tomb by Joseph of Arimathea, basically as the Gospels teach. But then someone, likely Joseph himself, would have moved the body quite soon afterward. It should be carefully noted that this has nothing to do with "stealing" the body of Jesus. According to this view, Jesus' body was simply moved to a different tomb in an orderly fashion. Then after the flesh had decayed, his bones would have been placed in the Talpiot ossuary.[6]

But this appears to involve a rather bizarre

sequence of events that never would have been concocted unless one were trying specifically to bridge the two stories and make the Talpiot Tomb the burial place of Jesus of Nazareth. It certainly does not make the best sense of what we know about Jesus' burial.

To begin, why would Joseph rebury the body in the same sort of tomb that Jesus' body had already been placed in? One could postulate that he simply wanted to keep the first one open for his own family or for other personal reasons. At this point, however, we should hark back to our earlier commitment to work with the data widely recognized by scholars, unless we have strong reasons for doing otherwise. Clearly we have no good reasons to think that Jesus' body was reburied within a day or so after his death, and later given a third burial in the ossuary, unless the entire point is to get Jesus' bones into the Talpiot Tomb! There is simply no data that would support this scenario.

Before moving on, one other issue needs to be mentioned. Biblical archaeologist Jodi Magness concludes that one can accept the explanation that Jesus was raised from the dead, or one can postulate that Jesus' body was reburied the most common way that it was done in first-century Israel—in a trench grave. This would involve placing the shrouded body in a rectangular opening in the earth. But, "Whatever explanation one prefers . . . his bones could not have been collected in an ossuary, at least not if we follow the Gospel accounts."[7]

Tabor is not sure whether or not Joseph would have told others about his reburial.[8] But would Joseph, an honorable man who was just trying to do the best thing for Jesus, never have informed anyone of his decision? At the very least, it is highly unlikely that he moved Jesus' body by himself. And no one witnessed the removal, especially when Joseph was not even trying to be secretive about it? Assuming that he got help, perhaps from more than one other person, what prevented them from sharing that incredibly important information? If everyone kept it hidden for some reason, especially if they never told anyone including Jesus' mother and family, now the hypothesis seems to have migrated into some form of conspiracy and fraud. It becomes reminiscent of the old Egyptian stories that those who buried the Pharaohs had to be killed so as not to divulge the whereabouts of the tomb!

So because of these as well as other serious problems, let's suppose that Joseph told Jesus' family that he had moved the body. This seems most natural, after all, or even required, since if Jesus' bones showed up later in the family tomb, with his name scratched on the outside of the ossuary, we can assume that many family members were quite aware of it!

It makes the most sense that Joseph would have informed them before he actually moved the body. After all, in any culture and time, would a man who appears to be virtually unknown to a family simply move their son's or brother's body and not tell them beforehand? To fail to do so would be outrageously disrespectful!

But now we are left in a quandary. Why would the women, including Jesus' mother Mary, go to the vacated tomb on Sunday morning and think it significant that Jesus' body was no longer there! And even if Joseph straightened out the matter upon hearing of their mistake, how can we account for the rise of even their initial faith in the resurrection? But we must move on.

The empty tomb is such a problem for Tabor, that when he gets to some of the sticky questions he simply "punts" and says that we can say no more because of the theological nature of the Gospels. No only is this assertion problematic in terms of the most recent New Testament studies, but by this time in the discussion, Tabor has already borrowed from the Gospels whenever he wants to make the points he needs. For example, he assumes the general crucifixion and burial scenarios, the person of Joseph of Arimathea, the time of the day and the hasty nature of Jesus' burial, the nature of the rock tomb and the stone rolled in front, and on and on.[9] But when these exact same sources destroy one's hypothesis, he opts out of the process!

Perhaps the greatest problem so far for the Talpiot Reburial Hypothesis is that the evidence for the empty tomb is so strong. Indeed, Tabor concedes it, saying that it is too difficult to make sense of the data without this truth.[10] But as we have seen, the empty tomb alone plays havoc with the Talpiot thesis. The following problems have to be solved, without any evidence on their behalf:

✖ There is no known reason why Joseph had to rebury the body of Jesus within 24 hours.

✖ If Jesus' body were reburied the most common way—in a trench grave—it's highly probable that no remains would have ever been placed in a family tomb. But what is the point of moving a body from one tomb to another?

✖ If Joseph never told anyone, how would he keep it from becoming known, especially given that he would presumably need help from others and that the process itself would likely gather attention?

✖ If Joseph did tell others, especially the family, why did Mary the mother of Jesus and others come to the tomb on Sunday morning and have no idea where Jesus' body was located?

> "IT IS VERY UNLIKELY THAT THE EARLIEST PALESTINIAN CHRISTIANS COULD CONCEIVE OF ANY DISTINCTION BETWEEN RESURRECTION AND PHYSICAL, 'GRAVE EMPTYING' RESURRECTION. TO THEM AN ANASTASIS WITHOUT AN EMPTY GRAVE WOULD HAVE BEEN ABOUT AS MEANINGFUL AS A SQUARE CIRCLE."
>
> E. EARLE ELLIS [11]

On what grounds do we accept the majority of the Gospel textual attestation to Jesus' death and burial, but stop short when it clearly fails to support our beloved hypotheses?

The Resurrection Appearances of Jesus

Whether they consider themselves liberal, moderate, or conservative, scholars often agree on a fair amount of details from the life of Jesus and the beginning of the early church. For example, the vast majority of scholars today think, at the very least, that Jesus' disciples along with others thought that they had seen appearances of the risen Jesus.[12]

Why is this crucial fact conceded by virtually all scholars, even skeptics? There are many reasons, but there are several major ones.

 The starting point is almost always Paul's eyewitness testimony that he had seen the risen Jesus, converting him from a life of persecuting Christian believers (1 Cor. 9:1; 15:8–10).

 Equally important is that this is set in the context of the early creedal material that Paul had received and passed on to others (1 Cor. 15:3–7). Most critical scholars think that this information dates from immediately after the crucifixion and that Paul received it in the early to mid-30s AD from Peter and James the brother of Jesus during his visit to Jerusalem (Gal. 1:13–20) that came approximately three years after Paul's conversion.

 Further, Paul took great care to check out his gospel message again with Peter, James the brother of Jesus, and John, and they confirmed his gospel, adding nothing (Gal. 2:1–10).

✳ Paul testified that the other apostles were teaching the same message that he was regarding the resurrection appearances of Jesus (1 Cor. 15:11–14).

Other reasons also point to the disciples' conviction that they had seen the risen Jesus.

✳ Many other creedal texts that date from the earliest period of Christianity also confirm these conclusions.

✳ James the brother of Jesus was an unbelieving skeptic until he also saw or thought that he saw an appearance of the risen Jesus (1 Cor. 15:7).

✳ The disciples were willing to die specifically for their message of the resurrection of Jesus, which demonstrates that they were totally convinced that it was true.

Christ in Emmaus (detail) by Rembrandt (1648).

✠ The empty tomb, discussed above, indicates that what happened to Jesus happened to his body, so this also points in the direction of actual appearances of the risen Jesus.[13]

These eight arguments are accepted by most scholars, and they point quite strongly to the fact that we have been addressing: the earliest disciples were utterly convinced that they had witnessed appearances of the risen Jesus. Further, most scholars agree that alternative attempts to explain away the resurrection on natural grounds also fail. If this is so, then the disciples were correct about what they thought they had seen: appearances of the risen Jesus.

In other words, the evidence indicates that the disciples thought that Jesus was alive and that they had seen him. If natural events do not explain these experiences, then the resurrection appearances become the best explanation. So the experiences plus the absence of natural alternatives equals the resurrection appearances!

We should mention once again that we are not saying that these facts are true simply because they are reported in the New Testament. If that were the basis for these events, then skeptical scholars who reject the inspiration or even the reliability of Scripture would presumably also reject these data. But virtually all scholars think that the disciples had real experiences that they thought were Jesus' resurrection appearances. It is rare to discover any scholars who deny this. That is because, as we said above, there are many reasons to accept these facts as historical. That is why so many scholars agree with them.

The Talpiot Tomb and the Risen Jesus

Therefore, we have to ask how the Talpiot Tomb Hypothesis fares against these accredited historical data. It did not do a very good job of answering the burial data. How does it address the subject of the resurrection appearances? My contention is that it does an even poorer job here.

According to any burial scenario that we have mentioned above, Mary the mother of Jesus must have been told, sooner or later, that Jesus had been reburied and later had his bones placed in an ossuary in the family tomb. Thus she would have known that his body, at least, had not been raised from the dead. We said that it makes by far the most sense that, if Joseph of Arimathea had reburied Jesus' body, he would have informed Jesus' family so they would know where to find the bones in order to rebury them later in the family tomb. But it also makes the best sense that he informed them before he moved the body.

But in this case the women, including Mary and Mary Magdalene, now have no reason to go to the old

The Three Marys at Christ's Grave by Fra Angelico

tomb on Sunday morning in order to finish the burial, since it already had been completed by Joseph. Nor would they be surprised to find the tomb empty. But now we encounter the next problem—what do the two Marys think when they and other women see Jesus? We might be reminded here that even very critical scholars take this claim very seriously.[14] Needless to say, their conviction about the appearance would collide with their knowledge that Jesus' body, at that very moment, lay dead in another tomb.

Though it is unlikely that Joseph, a fairly obscure follower of Jesus, would decide totally on his own to move the body without telling the family and friends of Jesus, what if he did wait until later to inform them? This still does not dissolve the problem of the appearances to the women. Not only would they in all likelihood be present in the groups to which Jesus appeared (see Luke 24:33; John 20:17-18), but they are specifically mentioned as being present at the end of the 40 days of Jesus' appearances, right after the ascension (Acts 1:14). Even without these texts, to think that the female disciples like the two Marys would not be present when Jesus appeared during this time is simply shortsighted.

The point is that there is absolutely no question from the texts we have that Jesus' mother Mary and Mary Magdalene both were believers, thought they had also seen the risen Jesus, and supported the efforts of the early church. Yet if within a year or so (at the very longest) Jesus' bones would be reburied in the Talpiot Tomb, what would happen to their ongoing faith?

Every time they entered the family tomb in order to rebury a family member, they would have been confronted with the reality of Jesus' horrible death by crucifixion. Perhaps they would even have had to periodically move or step over Jesus' own ossuary. Since the predominant Jewish view was resurrection of the body, with the ossuaries themselves being a pointer to this ongoing belief in the importance of the human bones, how could the women go on believing that Jesus had been raised from the dead? And then what becomes of their firm belief that they had seen him alive after his death?

With James the brother of Jesus we have a different twist to the problem. As the presumed head of the family after the death of Jesus, he, too, would know where the family reburial tomb was located, and that Jesus' name was displayed on the outside of the box. James, as well, would almost have to trip repeatedly over, or at least pass by, his brother's bones in order to rebury additional family members during the intervening years before his own death. This is highly problematic, given the critical scholarly view that James had been converted from skepticism by a resurrection appearance of Jesus, which is also a clear case of the principle of embarrassment mentioned above. He went from believing Jesus was deranged to a profound faith change.[15]

As a pious Jew, James knew that Jesus' "body" was still interred in the family tomb! How, then, could Jesus have been raised from the dead? After all, his brother's bones were safe in the family tomb, awaiting the resurrection! But there are additional problems in James' case that were not present for the Marys.

Given Jesus' reburial and then his interment in the ossuary, what would account for James' conversion from skepticism? And even if he had become a believer because of Jesus' resurrection appearance to him, as held by the majority of scholars, then why did he keep believing upon discovering the truth about his brother's body and bones? After all, a few years after Jesus' death, James is still the pastor of the church in Jerusalem.[16] And if James is the author of the Epistle, written years after that, the Lord Jesus Christ is still described as "glorious" (2:1), waiting to come (5:7) and preparing to judge (5:9). One last item about James should also be mentioned. If the recently-discovered James ossuary is authentic,[17] it might actually work against the Talpiot Tomb Hypothesis. The ossuary designation of "James son of Joseph brother of Jesus" would arguably indicate that, until his death, James was still identified with Christianity. This would confirm both the New Testament witness as well as the testimony of Josephus, who recorded James' martyrdom in Jerusalem.[18] Further, the ossuary inscription is a hint of Jesus' resurrection, for if James, for any reason, thought that Jesus had not been raised from the dead and was therefore less than the Lord,[19] it would seem that he would no longer be so identified in his death.[20] The bones in Talpiot would have cried out for a different kind of response.

We must move on now to one other very serious problem that the early conviction of resurrection appearances produces for the Talpiot Hypothesis.

Whenever Jesus' mother Mary, Mary Magdalene, and James found out about the reburial of Jesus' body, it would have to be no later than a year or so after the crucifixion, occasioned by the burial of his bones in the Talpiot family tomb. But this would be only a year or so into the life of the Christian church. How could this information possibly stay hidden from the apostles and other early leaders? One would think that the effect on the faith of at least these three early leaders would be devastating!

And as soon as the secret leaked out, how would

The Apostle Paul by Rublev.

the early proclamation of the gospel—the deity, death, and resurrection of Jesus—be affected? The truth of Jesus' reburial would hit the movement right between the eyes, at its very center! How would it affect Peter? John? Others?

Then of course, what do we do with Paul's conversion, based on what he thought was a resurrection appearance of Jesus? With Jesus dead, and with his body and bones already reburied by this time, does the Talpiot Hypothesis reveal any new insights regarding Paul's conversion? It would seem that this subject is not even addressed. Therefore, a different approach is needed here. It is far from clear that there is anything new to say about what changed Paul from a fearsome persecutor to a believer in Jesus Christ. But this change must be accounted for, due to the central nature of Paul's experience and his early resurrection report. It is certain that, as a former Pharisee (Phil. 3:5-6), Paul believed in resurrection of the body, as they did. This is further evidenced from his writings.[21]

Of course, the response from the Talpiot Hypothesis advocates might be that this is not a thesis about Paul. But since the Talpiot scenario does propose to be a fairly comprehensive contribution to the question of Christian origins, and reflecting on Jesus' resurrection in particular, we simply note that the issue of Paul's conversion cannot be sidestepped in this manner. What happened to Paul is near the center of Christianity. By not addressing this question well, and thereby emphasizing its lack of response to Paul's conversion, the Talpiot Hypothesis shows that it lacks explanatory power, a key ingredient of historical research. Therefore, it is weakened further.

All the evidence we have strongly opposes the Talpiot thesis here, and very firmly so. For example, during that initial meeting in Jerusalem mentioned above (Gal. 1:18-20), perhaps six years after the crucifixion, Paul, Peter, and even James (who knew "the truth" about Jesus at least years earlier[22]) met to discuss their shared Christian hope. Fourteen years later, they all met again, this time along with John, in order to discuss the nature of the gospel, concerning which they agreed. The result was a renewed effort to continue their missionary effort with more zeal than ever (Gal. 2:1-10).

There is not the slightest sign that any of them thought that they might be mistaken, or were less than totally committed to the truth of this message. Indeed, very early first-century sources tell us that James, Paul, and Peter died as martyrs for the gospel that they preached,[23] which included the central truth of Jesus' resurrection. This means, at the very least, that they believed their gospel message to the very end of their lives. This is simply devastating evidence against the Talpiot Hypothesis.

We must add quickly here what we are not saying. We are not saying that those who hold to the Talpiot Hypothesis will have nothing whatsoever to say. They will no doubt come up with some ideas that address a few of the many concerns raised in this book, or this chapter, in particular. But the key here is whether their scenarios are of the "what if" or "could be" types of solutions, like what Tabor presents,[24] or ones that follow the historical evidence that we know. As we have said, the evidence

The Resurrection by Matthias Grünewald (1515)

opposes them at virtually every turn. That is precisely why the almost wholesale scholarly reaction has been to reject their thesis.

One response that they have already made is to argue that Christians can still hold to a spiritual resurrection, without believing that Jesus' body was actually raised from the dead. But the problems with such a scenario are simply immense. This presupposes that the Talpiot Tomb suppositions are established, when they are hardly even live options after everything is said and done. Further, this was not the view of the New Testament writers[25] and we must account for their teachings, due to the powerful evidence in favor of them.

From the beginning, the earliest proclamation was the unwavering belief that Jesus had appeared to his followers—that he was seen by them. Further, the latest indications are that the Greek words that they used always meant that it was the body that was raised, not the spirit alone. The words were used in this way by everyone— pagans, Jews, and Christians alike. So the claim definitely was not that he was somehow spiritually alive. Rather, both individuals and groups claimed to have seen him, and this is hardly even questioned in the critical scholarly literature. The point is that we must account for the teachings themselves, not invent another scenario instead. Since the data we have supports this view, it simply must be addressed, not sidestepped. So the spiritual resurrection claim fails from the outset.[26]

Now we must summarize the issue in this chapter. We must add to the earlier list of burial problems for the Talpiot Hypothesis, this time from the known historical facts regarding the disciples' conviction that they had seen the risen Jesus, including their subsequent transformations and martyrdoms for the gospel message. Here is the other half of the major problems:

   Since the predominant Jewish view was that of bodily resurrection, further demonstrated specifically by the ossuary process itself and the particular word usage, knowing that Jesus' body and bones had never been raised would be an insurmountable barrier to the early resurrection faith.

✠ How could Jesus' mother Mary and Mary Magdalene reconcile their appearances of the risen Jesus with their knowledge that his body and bones had been reburied?

✠ How can we account for both James' conversion from skepticism as well as his work through the remainder of his life as pastor of the Jerusalem church when he also knew that his brother Jesus' bones were in the family tomb?

✠ To suppose that word of Jesus' reburial by Joseph and later interment in the ossuary never leaked out to the disciples is simply too much to ask.

✠ The Talpiot Hypothesis fails to address and account for Paul's conversion, which occurred after the ossuary reburial.

✠ The preaching zeal of Jesus' chief apostles, followed by their recorded martyrdoms, indicates that they believed to the very end, which hardly seems likely if they had knowledge of the reburials.

Conclusion

The Talpiot Tomb Hypothesis fails on virtually every major claim that it makes. Scarcely has a view ever been confronted by more major refutations than this one. And seldom has the scholarly community—skeptical, liberal, moderate, and conservative alike—joined ranks and reacted with almost a single voice. In fact, a quick survey indicates that more critical scholars seem to be leading the charge even more than their evangelical counterparts. "You are refuted by the known evidence" could be the clarion cry that has arisen time and again. The downright disgust with which several of these critical scholars have retorted has been surprising. In light of virtually all the facts that formulate the starting point for contemporary scholarship, there can be very little doubt that the Talpiot Hypothesis was tried in the scholarly courts and found wanting! The secret of the Talpiot Tomb has been known for two millennia: "He is not here. He is risen" (Matt. 28:6).

Notes

1. For just two examples of this approach as applied to the resurrection of Jesus, see Gary R. Habermas, *The Historical Jesus: Ancient Evidence for the Life of Christ* (Joplin, Mo: College Press, 1996); Habermas with Michael R. Licona, *The Case for the Resurrection of Jesus* (Grand Rapids: Kregel Publications, 2004). These and other texts may be consulted for much of the discussion in this chapter.

2. Matt. 28:11-15; Justin Martyr, *Dialogue with Trypho*, 108; Tertullian, *On Spectacles*, 30. Also, a Jewish writing from much later, the Toledoth Jesu, presents a similar account (Habermas, The Historical Jesus, 205–206; cf. Maier below, 200–202).

3. For many details on the Jewish view, see especially N.T. Wright, *The Resurrection of the Son of God* (Minneapolis: Fortress, 2003), chapters 3–5.

4. Paul L. Maier, *In the Fullness of Time: A Historian Looks at Christmas, Easter, and the Early Church* (San Francisco: Harper Collins, 1991), 197.

5. When scholars count source attestation, they do not simply count the Gospels as four independent texts. They count what they perceive to be the number of different reports from which the various Gospel accounts were derived. On the empty tomb, depending on the scholar, we have anywhere from three to six very early sources. Besides the three to four sources that scholars think they can find in the Gospel texts at this point, we also have the potential early creedal statement in Acts 13:29–30, 35–37, and the implications of Paul's early creedal report in 1 Corinthians 15:3–5. This does not even count the later but still useful reports by Justin Martyr and Tertullian.

6. James D. Tabor, "Two Burials of Jesus of Nazareth and

the Talpiot Yeshua Tomb," SBL Forum, 1–2.

7. Jodi Magness, "Has the Tomb of Jesus Been Discovered?" Biblical Archaeology Review, 3/5, 3.

8. Ibid, 2.

9. Tabor, "Two Burials of Jesus of Nazareth and the Talpiot Yeshua Tomb," 1–2, 4.

10. Ibid, 1–2.

11. Quoted in "Contemporary Scholarship and the Historical Evidence for the Resurrection of Jesus Christ," William Lane Craig, Truth Journal, http://www.leaderu.com/truth/1truth22.html

12. For many details, besides the sources above, see Gary R. Habermas, "Experiences of the Risen Jesus: The Foundational Historical Issue in the Early Proclamation of the Resurrection," Dialog: A Journal of Theology, Vol. 45 (Fall, 2006), 288–297; Gary R. Habermas, "Resurrection Research from 1975 to the Present: What Are Critical Scholars Saying?" Journal for the Study of the Historical Jesus, Vol. 3 (2005), 135–153.

13. For this list in a slightly different form, see Habermas, "Experiences of the Risen Jesus: The Foundational Historical Issue in the Early Proclamation of the Resurrection," 289–293.

14. Robert W. Funk and the Jesus Seminar, *The Acts of Jesus: The Search for the Authentic Deeds of Jesus* (S.F.: Harper Collins, 1998), 454; Helmut Koester, History and Literature of Early Christianity, Vol. 2 of Introduction to the New Testament (Philadelphia: Fortress, 1982), 84.

15. Compare Mark 3:21 and John 7:5 with 1 Cor. 15:7.

16. See Gal. 1:18–19; 2:1; Acts 15:13–21.

17. As noted above, this is disputed. See Hershel Shanks and Ben Witherington, *The Brother of Jesus* (San Francisco: Harper Collins, 2004).

18. Josephus, Antiquities of the Jews, 20:9:1.

19. The Epistle refers to Jesus as "Lord" and "Christ" (James 1:1; 2:1).

20. See the thesis of Shanks and Witherington, above.

21. See Habermas and Licona, chapter 9.

22. Jesus' bones should have been buried in the family tomb about five years earlier. I address James Tabor's objection in *Buried Hopes or Risen Savior? The Search for the Jesus Tomb*

edited by Charles L. Quarles, B&H Publishing Group, 2008.

23. For James' martydom, see Josephus, *Antiquities of the Jews*, 20:9:1. For Peter's and Paul's martyrdom, see Clement of Rome, Corinthians 5.

24. Especially in Tabor, "Two Burials of Jesus of Nazareth and the Talpiot Yeshua Tomb."

25. We must remember here what we said at the outset of this chapter. Our point is assuredly not that their view is wrong because the New Testament says so. The point is that with all the evidence that we have in support of the historical facts that we are using here, they are mistaken precisely because their hypothesis is refuted by that data at every turn. This is why virtually all scholars have reacted so strongly against their ideas.

26. I have addressed the possibility of a spiritual resurrection in the Appendix.

A SPIRITUAL RESURRECTION?

The Talpiot Hypothesis does not rule out actual resurrection appearances of Jesus, except to argue that such events would not involve Jesus' body that had been crucified. We will address two issues here: Could Jesus still have been raised from the dead? What sort of resurrection appearances do the data most support?

Was Jesus Raised from the Dead?

We addressed this question is some detail in the last chapter. Although brief, eight lines of evidence were suggested, accepted by the vast majority of scholars. Additionally, many more detailed arguments were referenced in the notes.[1] These separate strands produce a tight, detailed historical argument for the resurrection. Such data have changed the contemporary critical view in the direction of this event. Truly, nothing of this nature exists in other religious literature.

Here we simply want to add an addendum to that discussion. All lines of evidence argue that Jesus' disciples thought that they had seen the risen Jesus. Scholars who otherwise differ strongly on the import of these appearances are agreed that the disciples thought they had seen Jesus.

Although it would not be the traditional Christian answer, I simply want to make the point here that if Jesus was raised from the dead and appeared to his followers, either in a transformed body, or even as a glorified spiritual being, he would still actually have been raised from the dead. Thus, the Talpiot hypothesis, even if true, decisively fails to disprove Jesus' resurrection. All the data show that Jesus was seen again after his death, and since natural theses have failed,[2] the resurrection is strongly warranted. But unfortunately for the Talpiot view, their position fails on its own merits, for dozens of reasons.

How Did Jesus Appear?

Even by postulating the prospect of a spiritual resurrection, the Talpiot Hypothesis fails. Not only have they not ruled out an actual resurrection, as just mentioned, but an incredible amount of data point to Jesus being raised bodily, in the same body that was crucified, although there were definitely some incredibly wonderful changes. Here we will be able only to list some of these arguments.[3] It is crucial to bear in mind that we are only asking about the mode of Jesus' appearance. The entire argument turns on what the early sources taught with regard to what was seen. Simply asked, did they think Jesus' raised body appeared? Or was he a disembodied, glorious spirit?[4]

Outlined Arguments for Jesus' Bodily Resurrection Appearances

1. The predominant Jewish view in the First Century CE is that of bodily resurrection, so this forms a helpful backdrop for our discussion.
2. Paul placed himself squarely in this traditional Jewish position by identifying with the Pharisees (Phil. 3:4-6), a group that held to a bodily resurrection.[5]
3. N.T. Wright has shown in hundreds of pages of painstaking research that the chief terms for

resurrection always signify a bodily event. In fact, for hundreds of years before and after Jesus, until about 200 CE, regardless of whether pagans, Jews, or Christians used the terms, they always indicated bodily occurrences.[6]

4. As argued by Robert Gundry, the term "body" in the New Testament and other Jewish literature, and for Paul in particular, clearly refers to a physical organism. This is especially true of Paul's view of Jesus' resurrection appearances.[7]

5. In eleven centuries before and after Jesus, with one possible exception that is still quite unlikely, "spiritual body" never means an "immaterial body."[8]

6. Paul answers the question by using a term in Philippians 3:11 (cf. also 1 Cor. 15:12) that signifies being raised out from the realm of the dead, specifically indicating that his body would be raised. In 3:20-21, he asserts that Jesus would transform the believer's body to be like Jesus' glorious body (cf. also Rom. 8:11).

7. Paul's sociology also indicates bodily resurrection. He always refers to the resurrection of the dead in the plural, indicating a corporate event; believers would be raised together. And the realm of resurrection is the transformed earth (Rom. 8:18-23). These are very difficult concepts for glorified spirits!

8. Paul reports group appearances of Jesus (1 Cor. 15:4-7; cf. the creedal statement in Acts 13:30-31), which are more indicative of bodily events.

9. Every Gospel resurrection account clearly describes a bodily appearance of Jesus, including the continuity of crucifixion scars and the offer to inspect His body.

10. An empty tomb strongly implies bodily appearances.

Notes

1. For example, see the volume by Habermas and Licona, *The Case for the Resurrection of Jesus*.

2. For the hallucination and other similar views, see Gary R. Habermas, "Explaining Away Jesus' Resurrection: The Recent Revival of Hallucination Theories," *Christian Research Journal*, Vol. 23 (2001), pp. 26-31, 47-49. (See www.garyhabermas.com under "Articles.")

3. The sources in the last chapter will also provide additional details for these points.

4. Many of our points concern Paul's view, for it is by far the chief critical focus. That the Gospels teach bodily resurrection appearances is not challenged.

5. In Acts 23:6-9, Luke reports that Paul claimed to still be a Pharisee, specifically identifying with their view of bodily resurrection.

6. Wright, *The Resurrection of the Son of God*, pp. 32-552.

7. Robert Gundry, *Sōma in Biblical Theology, with Emphasis on Pauling Anthropology* (Cambridge: Cambridge University Press, 1976), especially chapter 13: "The Sōma in Death and Resurrection." Cf. Wright, pp. 263-264.

8. Michael Licona, "The Risen Jesus: Casper or Corporeal?" in Charles L. Quarles, *Buried Hopes or Risen Savior: The Search for Jesus' Tomb* (Nashville: B & H Publishing Group, 2008).

HOW SHOULD WE TREAT NEW CHALLENGES TO THE CHRISTIAN FAITH?

Challenges seem to arise every year in the popular press, often during the Christmas holidays. But more recently, the Easter season has been the designated time to break the bombastic news. Amid the twists and turns, expect the story to emerge in a similar manner—often as a news flash, promising exciting new evidence, scholarly opinion, and perhaps even photos or DNA testing.

In recent years, believers have been challenged with many questions. Was Jesus married to Mary Magdalene? Did Jesus father one or more children? Was Mary supposed to be the appointed leader of the church, but was denied that right by the male leaders? Was Judas Iscariot not really the betrayer of Jesus, but Jesus' key disciple? Was Christianity the invention of a Roman Emperor, centuries after the time of Jesus? Most recently, were Jesus' bones really discovered in his family's burial tomb? Was this proven by DNA tests?

Conversely, these objections can arise in other forms, too. Besides books and media presentations, the objections could more simply emerge from a newspaper, email, a discussion over coffee, or in other casual talks with friends.

Perhaps the majority of Christians would be

unbothered, responding by simply rolling their eyes and making comments about the current state of prejudice against believers. But others may react fearfully, as if their faith were in danger of crumbling at any moment. This latter response seems to be an initial reaction, rarely based on actual studies of the claims themselves.

How ought Christians to respond to ideas which, if they were true, might undermine their faith to various extents? We will propose some general suggestions that might be utilized during the process of evaluation. These ideas can be adjusted or applied as needed.

1) Divorce the challenge from our emotions. By analogy, believers who react with immediately elevated emotions may seem like the new car that accelerates from 0 to 60 in six seconds! Too often, these emotions are completely unwarranted in terms of the data, as indicated a few days or weeks later, when everything has calmed down and returned to normal. After all, how many sensationalistic claims have been made over the years? Have any of them been devastating? This is one clue.

Even if it initially appears like there may be some substance to the claim, there is still no reason to connect one's emotions to the issue. Many researchers have noted that this sort of emotional quandary is linked, not to the challenges themselves, but to the things that we say to ourselves about the challenges. For example, if we tell ourselves such catastrophic things as, "Oh no, what if my faith is misplaced?" or "What if the Bible is wrong?" such statements will often cause very strong emotions. These feelings can actually arise mere moments after the errant thoughts.

So we need to begin with more calming thoughts. True, a challenge may have been proposed. Now let's study the claims that are being made.

2) Know the basis for Christian Theism. Jousting with the various challenges to faith presupposes that we know at least the basic reasons that undergird that belief structure. Too many Christians attempt to counter critical views without having done their own homework, only to become part of the problem when they also seek advice and counseling!

Part of knowing the basis for Christian Theism involves working from the center out. In other words, the closer a doctrine or area of practice is to the foundations of Christianity, the more it needs to be buttressed. Correspondingly, questions on periphery areas of the faith do not need to be treated with the same sort of diligence as attacks on indispensable doctrines. After all, Christians differ with each other on some of these same points! But it is no coincidence that our cardinal doctrines are also the best-grounded beliefs, often established by multi-faceted cases. We must remember that since the center holds firmly, we should rest securely.

3) Think through each critical premise in light of an overall strategy. When we do respond, we should think through each portion of our opponent's argument, giving the most weight and attention to the areas of the opposing position that are the most crucial. For instance, which of the opposing premises, if successfully challenged, would count most heavily against the entire critical thesis? Another relevant, though somewhat less important question, concerns which assertions are the most open to counterattack?

Second only to knowing the basis for Christian Theism, we should also understand and use some of the basic principles of critical thinking. Some scholars exhibit an almost uncanny knack for dissecting opposing arguments and exposing their most crucial weaknesses. This trait can often be learned and should thus be cultivated. One way to do this is to study the tapes, books, and articles of those who debate well. The experience can be similar to watching a chess match. What overall strategy is being pursued? Why did they make certain moves? Were there still better arguments at their disposal? In short, there is no substitute for knowing the data and then being able to use it effectively.

As already mentioned, we likewise want to defend most clearly those areas that are most central to our own thesis. It is at this precise intersection of challenging our opponent's chief arguments as they most impact the heart of Christian theism that we make our strongest stand. This is where we both pour on the relevant data, while employing the best argumentative techniques.

4) Restate the total case. When we are finished with our critique, we should put the pieces back together. In discussions of this nature, many people lose focus on the most crucial elements and often feel that they have lost contact with the "real" points being made. Therefore, we can encourage everyone involved by restating and clarifying the chief points in favor of Christian Theism, as well as the best critiques against the opposing position.

In sum, divorcing critical challenges from our emotions is a prerequisite to treating the actual questions. Then there are no substitutes for knowing our own position and for having the basic tools involved in digesting and dissecting an argument. These tools provide the basis upon which we build our counter-challenge, aiming for the most crucial and vulnerable premises of our opponents' position. The result should be a carefully-reasoned, final case that clearly showcases the truth of Christian Theism.

FOR MORE ON THE TALPIOT HYPOTHESIS...

EDITED BY CHARLES L. QUARLES

BURIED HOPE *or* RISEN SAVIOR

THE SEARCH FOR THE JESUS TOMB

BURIED HOPE OR RISEN SAVIOR? THE SEARCH FOR THE JESUS TOMB

EDITED BY CHARLES L. QUARLES

Not long after the announcement that the Jesus Family Tomb had been discovered in a suburb of Jerusalem, Charles Quarles felt that a carefully-reasoned response was needed.

"I quickly realized that no single scholar possessed the wide-range of expertise necessary to fully address the claims of The Jesus Family Tomb. I am a New Testament scholar who specializes in Gospel study and historical Jesus research, but I am not an archaeologist and certainly not a statistician. I began putting together a "dream team" of evangelical scholars including an archaeologist, a statistician, an expert on Jewish ossuaries, New Testament and historical Jesus scholars so that each major claim of the hypothesis could be addressed by a true expert in that respective field. Richard Bauckham, Darrell Bock, William Dembski, Craig A. Evans, Gary Habermas, Mike Licona, Robert Marks, and Steve Ortiz committed to the project. The end result is Buried Hope or Risen Savior? The Search for the Jesus Tomb, the most comprehensive scholarly response to the Talpiot hypothesis to date."

Contents